Academic Writing Skills

Student's Book

1

Peter Chin   Yusa Koizumi   Samuel Reid

Sean Wray   Yoko Yamazaki

Shaftesbury Road, Cambridge CB2 8EA, United Kingdom

One Liberty Plaza, 20th Floor, New York, NY 10006, USA

477 Williamstown Road, Port Melbourne, VIC 3207, Australia

314–321, 3rd Floor, Plot 3, Splendor Forum, Jasola District Centre, New Delhi – 110025, India

103 Penang Road, #05-06/07, Visioncrest Commercial, Singapore 238467

Cambridge University Press is part of the University of Cambridge.

We share the University's mission to contribute to society through the pursuit of education, learning and research at the highest international levels of excellence.

www.cambridge.org

This is the revised and expanded edition of *Academic Writing Skills and Strategies I*, ISBN 978-4-903049-14-4 first published in Japan by Waseda University International Co., Ltd. in 2007

First published 2012

20 19 18

Printed in Great Britain by CPI Group (UK) Ltd, Croydon CR0 4YY

ISBN 978-1-107-63622-4 paperback Student's Book 1
ISBN 978-1-107-64293-5 paperback Teacher's Manual 1

Contributors: Joseph Garner, Adam Gyenes, Christopher Pellegrini, Dean Poland
Editor: Sean Wray

Cover photo: ©iStockphoto.com/pablohart

Academic Writing Skills has been developed by the Research and Development team at Waseda University International Co., Ltd., Tokyo.

Contents

How this book is organized

Academic Writing Skills 1 introduces the essential skills and strategies required to compose academic essays.

There are four units in the textbook:

- Unit 1: how to structure a paragraph – the basic building block for essays.
- Unit 2: from writing paragraphs to composing longer pieces of work (essays).
- Unit 3: how to paraphrase and summarize, and use information from outside sources.
- Unit 4: how to write a research essay, with particular focus on presenting opinions and supporting them with evidence.

Each unit presents explanations, examples, exercises, and model paragraphs and essays to help you attain a level of academic writing expected of university students.

Academic Writing Skills 1 also includes sections focusing on grammar and stylistic aspects of academic writing, such as how to use:

- conjunctions.
- transitional expressions.
- pronouns.

Studying these sections will enable you to express your thoughts accurately using appropriate language for academic writing.

The book also focuses on using sources and citation – one of the most important skills in academic writing. The information and exercises presented will help you learn how to:

- quote, paraphrase and summarize information from outside sources.
- effectively integrate this information in your essays.
- identify the sources of information in your essays using the appropriate format.

To maximize the use of this book, you should:

- read the information in each unit thoroughly.
- take notes in the page margins of ideas and explanations from your teacher, classmates, or your own thoughts.
- complete all the exercises.

Dedicated study of *Academic Writing Skills 1* will prepare you with the basic but necessary skills and strategies to successfully write academic essays.

Introduction to academic writing

What is academic writing?

Regardless of their major, university students are required to compose different types of writing, such as term papers or exam answers, throughout their studies. "Academic writing" is a general term that refers to all writing created for the purpose of study. University students are evaluated largely based on their writing, so writing skills are essential for academic success.

Academic writing is different from other types of writing in several ways.

1. Purpose

The main purpose of academic writing is to demonstrate knowledge of a topic. Certain writing tasks, however, have more specific purposes, such as:

- to explain a subject.
- to report research findings.
- to analyze and evaluate a subject.
- to express an opinion about an issue and persuade the reader to accept it.

2. Audience

"Audience" refers to the reader of your writing. In academic writing, your audience is usually the instructor of the course, who reads your essay and evaluates it. However, whenever you write, it is often useful to imagine that you are writing for a larger audience. This audience might:

- not know about the topic as thoroughly as your teacher does.
- have a background different from yours (e.g., is from another country) and thus not have the same values or experiences as you. Keeping this audience in mind will help you write so that your message is communicated clearly and powerfully.

3. Evidence

Evidence is an important feature of academic writing. Any claim or opinion from the writer must be supported with evidence, such as:

- examples.
- statistics.
- experts' opinions.

Without evidence, the writer's ideas might be considered unreliable or even biased.

If your evidence is information from outside sources, you must acknowledge the original source in your essay – in other words, use citation. Not citing outside information in your essay is called plagiarism. Plagiarism is considered stealing and is strictly forbidden.

4. **Style**

   In academic writing, you are expected to write in a certain style, which includes:

   - presenting ideas clearly and logically.
   - having organized paragraphs.
   - writing from a third person's point of view.
   - using formal language.

5. **The process of writing**

   Successful academic writing often cannot be achieved in one try. Certain steps should be followed before and after writing to ensure that ideas are presented effectively. A complete writing process might look like the following:

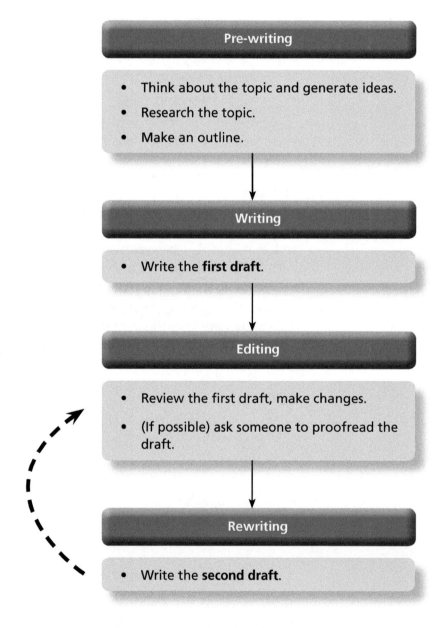

Becoming competent in each step of the writing process will lead to better writing. In fact, many writers repeat the last two steps (editing and rewriting) and write a third or fourth draft before completing the final version.

UNIT 1

Writing a Paragraph

1 Getting ready to write

The goals of this lesson:

- Identifying the structure of a paragraph
- Generating ideas for writing
- Writing a topic sentence
- Choosing supporting points
- Making an outline

Section 1 | What is a paragraph?

A **paragraph** is a group of sentences about a topic. Every paragraph should have one **topic**, which is usually presented in the first sentence called the **topic sentence**. All the other sentences in the paragraph must develop and support the topic.

When you write a paragraph, keep the topic in mind and try not to include sentences that are irrelevant (not directly related), which could confuse the reader.

Exercise 1 | **Read the model paragraph on the next page and answer the questions.**

1. What is the topic of the paragraph?

2. The paragraph has two irrelevant sentences. Find them and cross them out.

Reasons for Going to University

After graduating from high school, many students go on to university, but their reasons for entering higher education vary. First, many students attend university to study a particular subject in depth. Unlike high schools, which require students to take a wide range of classes, university curriculums allow students to choose a major. In each major, a number of specialized courses are offered, and they are taught by experts in the fields. Moreover, universities have various research facilities that help students learn. Another common reason for going to university is that a college education often leads to a better career in the future. In many countries, people with university degrees tend to find better-paying jobs than those without them. In addition, some universities provide their students with opportunities to acquire practical skills that can be useful in the real world, such as accounting, using computers, and speaking foreign languages. However, in spite of these opportunities, some students cannot find a rewarding job after graduation because of unfavorable economic conditions. Finally, for some students, making friends and enjoying an active social life can be a sufficient reason to stay in school for another four years. In universities, students have chances to meet people who come from different places with diverse backgrounds. Furthermore, universities have a variety of student organizations where students can meet others with similar interests and spend time with them. Sometimes students make friends through part-time jobs too. To sum up, students go to university for a variety of reasons: to study a particular field, to find a good job, or to make friends.

A paragraph is made up of three components: the **topic sentence**, the **supporting sentences** (body), and the **concluding sentence**.

Topic sentence
- The first sentence in a paragraph
- Presents the **topic** and the **controlling idea** (an important idea about the topic) of the paragraph

Supporting sentences
- The main part of the paragraph
- Provide several **supporting points** that explain the controlling idea of the paragraph
- Provide details that explain each supporting point

Concluding sentence
- The last sentence in a paragraph
- Restates the controlling idea and summarizes the supporting points

Exercise 2

Look at the model paragraph on page 3.

1. Identify the three components: the topic sentence, the supporting sentences, and the concluding sentence.

2. Answer the following questions.

   a. What is the controlling idea of the paragraph?
   b. How many supporting points are there in the paragraph? What are they?

Section 3 Generating ideas for writing – brainstorming

When you are given a writing task, the first thing you should do is to think about the topic and find ideas for your task. This activity is called **brainstorming**. Brainstorming can take many forms. You can brainstorm:

- on your own by writing down ideas on paper.
- with other people by discussing the topic.

Brainstorming is useful for timed essays, such as in tests, or for a writing task which does not require research. Below are some popular techniques for brainstorming.

1. Listing

Listing is an activity where you think about the topic and make a list of your ideas. When listing, remember:

- You can put all the ideas into a list like the one below, or you can classify them in groups.
- Do not reject any idea at this point because it might turn out to be useful later.

Reasons for going to university

- to study a particular subject
- to get a good job in the future
- to make friends
- to join a club
- to have fun
- to have free time before starting to work
- to think about the future
- to meet people from different places

---

2. Mind mapping

Mind mapping is another brainstorming activity. To draw a mind map:

1. Write the topic in the center of a blank sheet of paper.
2. Think of any word or phrase that is related to the topic and write it next to the topic.
3. Draw a line between the word and the topic.
4. Think of a new word related to either one of the two words on the sheet and write it down.
5. Continue until you have enough ideas.

One advantage of mind mapping is that relationships between ideas are visually displayed. This makes it easy for you to find clusters of ideas that are related to each other.

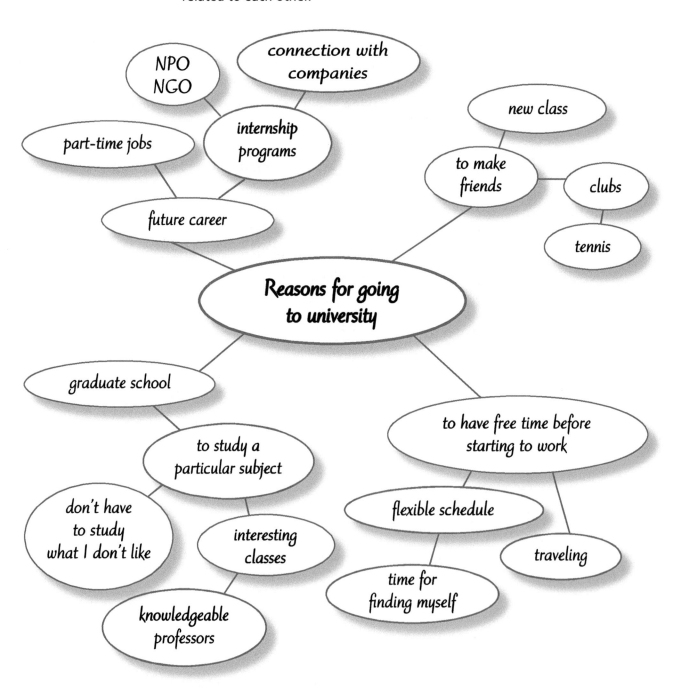

3. Free writing

Free writing is a brainstorming activity in which you:

1. think about the topic and write down your thoughts on a piece of paper.

2. keep writing whatever comes to mind for about ten minutes.

Remember, for free writing:

*   do not go back to rewrite your ideas.
*   do not worry about organization, grammar or style.
*   when you finish, read what you have written, and identify the ideas that will be useful for your task.

> Why do people go to university? Many people in my country go to university to enjoy themselves. Before university, students are busy studying for entrance exam. Some are busy with part-time jobs or school activities. After university, they are busy with work. There is no time to relax or think. So they go to university to relax and have fun with friends. Also to think about many things, for example future. We think about what we want to do, what kind of job we want to do in future and so on. But some people have more serious reason. To study something. If they have a subject they are interested. For example, I'm interested in cultures of other countries. I chose this university because there are famous professors and many interesting courses about Asian cultures, Islamic cultures, and so on. There is study abroad program too, so I can live in foreign country and experience culture of that country.

Exercise 3

Imagine you are asked to write a paragraph about one of these topics. Choose a topic and brainstorm ideas using one of the techniques described in this section.

1. Reasons for studying abroad

2. Advantages of joining a university student organization

3. Causes of stress among university students

4. Factors in choosing a university

5. Ways technology helps university students

Section 4 — Writing a topic sentence

After you decide which ideas to include in your paragraph, the next step in the writing process is to write a **topic sentence**. As you learned in Section 2, the topic sentence of a paragraph has two functions:

*   to introduce the **topic** of the paragraph.
*   to state the **controlling idea** of the paragraph.

The **controlling idea** is an important idea about the topic that the writer wants to convey in the paragraph. It is called the controlling idea because it limits or "controls" which information can be included in the paragraph. In other words, all the information in a paragraph must be relevant only to the controlling idea.

The topic sentence of the model paragraph on page 3 is:

After graduating from high school, many students go on to university, but their reasons for entering higher education vary.

This sentence gives the reader the following information about the paragraph:

Topic: Reasons for going to university

Controlling idea: Reasons for going to university vary

Note that there are many different ways to look at a topic, so the same topic can lead to different controlling ideas. See the following examples:

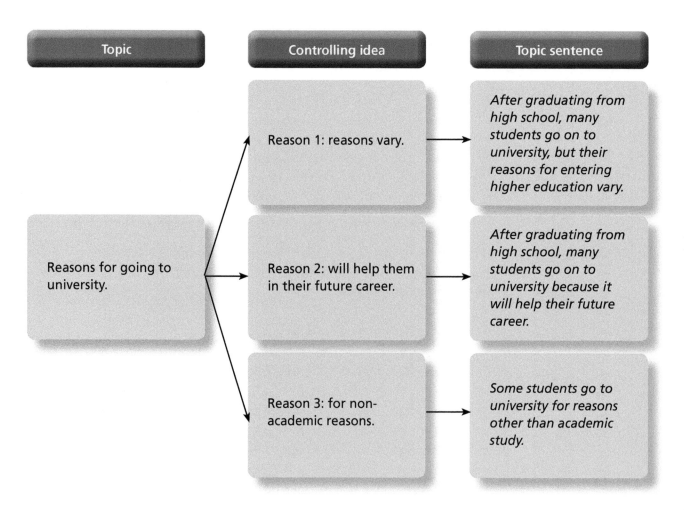

Topic	Controlling idea	Topic sentence
	Reason 1: reasons vary.	*After graduating from high school, many students go on to university, but their reasons for entering higher education vary.*
Reasons for going to university.	Reason 2: will help them in their future career.	*After graduating from high school, many students go on to university because it will help their future career.*
	Reason 3: for non-academic reasons.	*Some students go to university for reasons other than academic study.*

Therefore, when you write a paragraph, the first thing you should do is decide the controlling idea. Then, begin the paragraph with a sentence that presents both the topic and the controlling idea.

A good topic sentence is direct and concise. A sentence that is too general or too specific is not a good topic sentence. Compare the following topic sentences:

Topic: Reasons for going to university

Controlling idea: Reasons for going to university vary

Topic sentences:

✓ *After graduating from high school, many students go on to university, but their reasons for entering higher education vary.*

✗ *After graduating from high school, many students go on to university.* (too general)

✗ *After graduating from high school, many students go on to university mainly to study the subject they are interested in.* (too specific)

Exercise 4

Choose the best topic sentence for each controlling idea. Explain why the other choices are less appropriate.

1. **Topic:** Clubs at university

    Controlling idea: There are three types of clubs at university.

    Topic sentences:
    a. Universities usually have many sports clubs.
    b. University clubs can be classified into three types.
    c. Many university students enjoy club activities after their classes are over.

2. **Topic:** Living in a university dormitory

    Controlling idea: Living in a dormitory has many benefits for university students.

    Topic sentences:
    a. When students start university, some of them move into a dormitory.
    b. The main benefit of living in a dormitory is free air conditioning.
    c. Living in a dormitory brings a number of benefits to university students.

3. **Topic:** Academic writing skills for university students

    Controlling idea: Academic writing skills are essential for high grades in university.

    Topic sentences:
    a. Good academic writing skills help students in university and throughout their lives.
    b. In university, having academic writing skills is important to achieve good marks.
    c. The ability to write well is a requirement for top grades in literature.

After writing a topic sentence, you must choose several **supporting points** to include in your paragraph. These supporting points:

- must be relevant to the paragraph topic.
- provide examples or reasons that explain your controlling idea.
- must be sufficiently different from each other so that each one can be developed independently.

The model paragraph on page 3 has three supporting points. They support the controlling idea by providing three reasons for going to university.

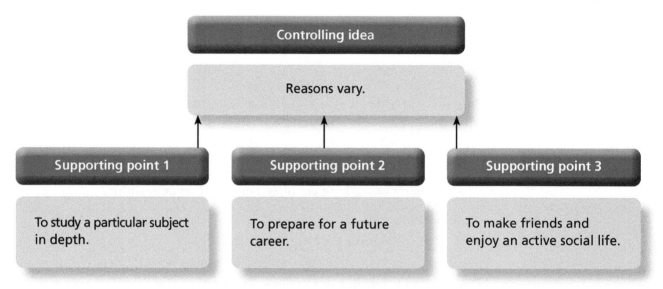

The example below shows a controlling idea which is more specific – how going to university will help students in their future career.

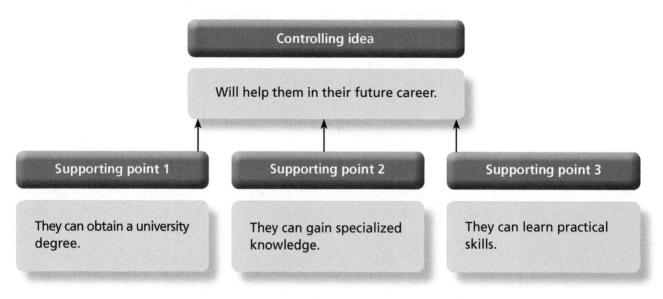

When you choose supporting points, it is a good idea to go back to the notes you made in the brainstorming activity. You can probably find good supporting points in these notes.

Section 6 — Making an outline

When you have written a topic sentence and selected supporting points, you should organize these ideas into an **outline** (see below).

Making an outline is essential because:

- it prevents you from going off topic and writing something irrelevant.
- you do not have to stop and think about the organization while you are writing.
- you can focus on grammar and style while you are writing because you do not have to think of ideas.

OUTLINE

Topic: Reasons for going to university

Topic sentence:
After graduating from high school, many students go on to university, but their reasons for entering higher education vary.

Supporting points:

1. To study a particular subject in depth

2. To prepare for a future career

3. To make friends and enjoy an active social life

Look at the notes you made in Exercise 3 (page 7). Using some of those ideas, write a topic sentence and choose three supporting points. Organize the ideas in the outline below.

OUTLINE

Topic: _____

Topic sentence:

_____

_____

_____

Supporting points:

1. _____

2. _____

3. _____

Review questions

1. What are the three components of a paragraph?

2. What are the three techniques of brainstorming?

3. What are the two functions of a topic sentence?

4. What are the benefits of making an outline?

Part 1

2 Writing a paragraph

The goals of this lesson:

- Supporting ideas with details
- Organizing supporting sentences
- Writing a concluding sentence
- Choosing a title
- Writing the first draft

Section 1   Supporting ideas with details

The function of the **supporting sentences** is to explain the controlling idea stated in the topic sentence. These supporting sentences consist of **supporting points** and specific **details**. The diagram below shows the relationships between the controlling idea, the first supporting point, and the details in the model paragraph about reasons for going to university (page 3).

Controlling idea

Reasons for going to university vary.

Supporting point 1

To study a particular subject in depth.

Detail a	Detail b	Detail c
Students can choose a major. High school students have to study a wide range of subjects.	Many specialized courses taught by experts.	Various research facilities.

You can use various types of information to support ideas in your paragraph, such as:

- reasons
- examples
- statistical evidence
- comparisons with other ideas

One way to find useful details is to ask yourself questions with *when, where, why* and *how*.

Exercise 1 **Read the model paragraph on page 3 again and identify the details used in the body. Add them to the outline below.**

OUTLINE

Topic: Reasons for going to university

Topic sentence:
After graduating from high school, many students go on to university, but their reasons for entering higher education vary.

Supporting points:

1. To study a particular subject in depth:

    a. Students can choose a major. High school students study a wide range of subjects.

    b. Many specialized courses taught by experts.

    c. Various research facilities.

2. To prepare for a future career:

    a. _____

    b. _____

3. To make friends and enjoy an active social life:

    a. _____

    b. _____

Section 2   Organizing supporting sentences

An average paragraph has six to ten supporting sentences. It is important to put them in logical order so that the reader can easily understand your ideas.

Follow these steps to organize your supporting sentences:
1.   Write one sentence to state the first supporting point.
2.   Write one or two sentences to provide details to support that point.
3.   Move on to the next supporting point.

Transitional expression

Supporting point 1

Details

Supporting point 2

Details

Supporting point 3

Details

After graduating from high school, many students go on to university, but their reasons for entering higher education vary. First, many students attend university to study a particular subject in depth. Unlike high schools, which require students to take a wide range of classes, university curriculums allow students to choose a major. In each major, a number of specialized courses are offered, and they are taught by experts in the fields. In addition, universities have research facilities that help students learn. Another common reason for going to university is that college education often leads to a better career in the future. In many countries, people with university degrees tend to find better-paying jobs than those without them. In addition, some universities provide their students with opportunities to acquire practical skills that can be useful in the real world, such as accounting, using computers, and speaking foreign languages. Finally, for some students, making friends and enjoying an active social life can be a sufficient reason to stay in school for another four years. In universities, students have chances to meet people who come from different places with diverse backgrounds. In addition, universities have a variety of clubs and other student organizations where students can meet those with similar interests and spend time with them. To sum up, students go to university for a variety of reasons: to study a particular field, to find a good job, or to make friends.

When introducing a new supporting point, writers often use a word such as *first*, *second*, *another*, and *finally*. These words are called **transitional expressions**. They show where one supporting point ends and another one begins. (You will learn more about transitional expressions in Unit 1, Part 3.)

Exercise 2 The following are sentences from a paragraph about the living situations of university students. Put each detail (right column) under the appropriate supporting point (left column). Make sure the details are in a logical order.

Topic sentence:

Living situations of university students can be classified into three types.

Supporting points	Details
1. First, students whose homes are close enough to school often live with their families. *e.*	a. Dormitory life often involves various constraints. b. However, they need to be independent and responsible because there is no one to take care of them. c. Students can be free from rules and restrictions in this living situation. d. For example, students have to cooperate with other residents and follow rules about leaving and returning, smoking and drinking, making noise and having guests.
2. Second, students who live too far away from school to commute might move into a dormitory.	e. Many students find this situation convenient because they can depend on their families for different kinds of housework such as cooking, cleaning, and doing the laundry.
3. Finally, living alone in an apartment is a popular choice among students who cannot commute to school from their homes but do not like the inconveniences of dormitory life.	f. Although these restrictions are sometimes inconvenient, they teach students important skills that might help them in the future. g. Some students, however, find it uncomfortable to be placed under the watchful eyes of their parents all the time.

Section 3   Writing a concluding sentence

The **concluding sentence** of a paragraph has two main functions:

- to restate the **controlling idea** given in the topic sentence.
- to summarize the **supporting points** discussed in the body.

For example, the following is the topic sentence and supporting points of the model paragraph about reasons for going to university:

Topic sentence: *After graduating from high school, many students go on to university, <u>but their reasons for entering higher education vary</u>.*

controlling idea

Supporting points:

1. To study a particular subject in depth.
2. To prepare for a future career.
3. To make friends and enjoy an active social life.

Compare this sentence to the concluding sentence of the paragraph:

restatement of controlling idea

To sum up, <u>students go to university for a variety of reasons</u>: <u>to study a particular field, to find a good job, or to make friends.</u>

summary of supporting points

The concluding sentence above:

- states the controlling idea given in the topic sentence using different words.
- presents again the three supporting points in the same order as they appear in the paragraph, but in different words.

Below are two more examples that show the relationship between the topic sentence, supporting points, and concluding sentence:

Example A

Topic sentence: *After graduating from high school, many students go on to university because it will help them in their future career.*

Supporting points:

1. They can obtain a university degree.
2. They can gain specialized knowledge.
3. They can learn practical skills.

Concluding sentence: *To summarize, with their degree, specialized knowledge, and practical skills, university graduates have an advantage in the job market, and for some students, this is the main reason for attending university.*

Example B

Topic sentence: *Some students go to university for reasons other than academic study.*

Supporting points:

1. To meet many people.
2. To enjoy sports and hobbies.
3. To find a better career in the future.

Concluding sentence: *In short, some students go to university not to study but to socialize with other students, participate in club activities, or to find a good job.*

NOTE: A concluding sentence often begins with a transitional expression for summarizing, such as *in short, to summarize,* or *to sum up.*

Exercise 3

For each of the following examples, write a concluding sentence that restates the controlling idea in the topic sentence and summarizes the supporting points.

1. **Topic sentence:** University clubs can be classified into three types.

    Supporting points:
    1. Sports
    2. Arts
    3. Academic

    Concluding sentence:

    _____

    _____

    _____

2. **Topic sentence:** Living in a dormitory brings a number of benefits to university students.

    Supporting points:
    1. They can make friends.
    2. They can learn social skills.
    3. They can save money.

    Concluding sentence:

    _____

    _____

    _____

3. **Topic sentence:** Good academic writing skills help students in several ways in university and beyond.

Supporting points:
1. They help students complete university assignments successfully.
2. They lead to good grades.
3. They help students in their future career.

Concluding sentence:

_____

_____

_____

Exercise 4

Write a concluding sentence for the paragraph you outlined in Exercise 5 in Unit 1, Part 1 (page 12).

_____

_____

_____

Section 4   Choosing a title

A piece of writing should have a title. A title should:
- let the reader know the topic of the writing.
- not be too long nor too general.

Compare the following examples:

Topic: Reasons for going to university

Title:

✓   *Why Students Go to University*

✗   *People Go to University for Three Different Reasons* (too long)

✗   *Going to University* (too general)

Topic: The different living situations of students at university

Title:

✓   *Living Situations of University Students*

✗   *Different Living Situations* (too general)

✗   *How to Live Comfortably* (off topic)

When you write a title, use capital letters correctly. See Appendix A (page 119) for the rules of capitalization.

Exercise 5

Choose the best titles for the topic sentences and supporting points in Exercise 3 (page 18). Explain why the other choices are less appropriate.

1. a. University Clubs
   b. Different Types of Clubs at University
   c. What Are Three Types of Clubs at University?

2. a. Benefits of Living in a University Dormitory
   b. Living in a Dormitory Has a Number of Benefits for University Students
   c. Wonderful Friendships in Dormitories

3. a. Good Academic Writing Equals Good Grades
   b. Information about Academic Writing
   c. The Importance of Academic Writing Skills for University Students

Section 5 — Writing the first draft

You are now ready to write the first draft of your paragraph. When you write the first draft, remember:
- Use your outline as you are writing.
- Focus on the ideas and how to organize them logically.
- The first draft is not the final product; you will have chances to improve it later, especially your grammar, choice of words, and style.

Review questions

1. What kind of information can you use to support your ideas in a paragraph?
2. How should you organize the supporting sentences?
3. What are the two functions of the concluding sentence?
4. What are the features of a good title?

3 | Writing a coherent paragraph

The goals of this lesson:

- Understanding coherence
- Using conjunctions
- Using transitional expressions
- Avoiding run-on sentences and sentence fragments

Section 1   Coherence

Coherence is an important quality of good writing. In a coherent paragraph, the reader can follow the writer's thoughts easily because:

- all the sentences are ordered logically.
- the transition from one sentence to another is smooth.
- the relationships between ideas are clearly shown.

There are several ways you can make your paragraph coherent:

- Organize supporting sentences in a logical order (See Unit 1, Part 2).
- Use conjunctions to show the relationship between ideas in the same sentence.
- Use transitional expressions to show the relationship between sentences.
- Use pronouns (See Unit 2, Part 3).

Conjunctions are words that combine two or more clauses into one sentence and show how the clauses relate to each other. For example, some conjunctions show how two clauses:

- are similar or different.
- have a cause-effect relationship.
- have a chronological (time) relationship.

Clauses

A clause is a group of words that contains a subject and a verb. There are two kinds of clauses: independent and dependent.

- An independent clause expresses a complete meaning and can stand alone as a sentence.
  Examples:
  Dormitory life involves various constraints.
  Some students study abroad.

- A dependent clause does not express a complete meaning and cannot exist on its own. It begins with a subordinating conjunction, and it has to be attached to an independent clause in order to make a grammatically correct sentence.
  Examples:
  ... although dormitory life involves various constraints.
  ... because they can develop foreign language skills.

There are two kinds of conjunctions: coordinating and subordinating.

1. Coordinating conjunctions

The coordinating conjunctions *for, and, nor, but, or, yet, so* join two independent clauses. A comma is placed between the first clause and the coordinating conjunction.

independent clause	+ comma + **coordinating conjunction** +	independent clause

*Working part-time gives students extra spending money, **and** it helps them learn about society.*

*Many smokers know about the risk of smoking, **but** they still cannot break the addiction.*

Relationship between clauses	Coordinating conjunction	Examples
Expresses a reason (**Note**: *for* is more commonly used as a preposition)	*for*	*Marta had to talk to her professor to arrange a make-up exam, **for** she missed the final exam.*
Expresses ideas or things that do not contrast	*and*	*Students can save money by living in a dormitory, **and** they can learn skills to get along with other people.*
Expresses negative ideas or things that do not contrast	*nor*	*The room in the dormitory did not have a private bathroom, **nor** did it have a kitchen.*
Expresses contrast or exceptions	*but*	*Emma wanted to go to a university in a different city, **but** she decided to go to the one in her hometown to stay with her family.*
Expresses an alternative	*or*	*Students who live in this dormitory can cook their own meal, **or** they can buy it at the cafeteria.*
Expresses (often unexpected) contrast or exceptions	*yet*	*Aisha was told that people in big cities were unfriendly, **yet** she found that they were as kind as people in her village.*
Expresses consequence	*so*	*There are hundreds of students in university, **so** it seems difficult to make friends at first.*

⚠ **Do not** use a coordinating conjunction to begin a sentence in academic writing.

NOTE: Coordinating conjunctions also join words and phrases (a group of words that does not contain both a subject and a verb).

Remember, when the coordinating conjunctions

• join two words or phrases, a comma is not necessary:

*Students have to take advanced <u>reading</u> **and** <u>writing</u> classes this semester.*
*When having a problem, students can <u>consult the course instructor</u> **or** <u>go to the writing center</u>.*

• join three or more words or phrases in a list, commas are used:

*When having a problem, students can <u>consult the course instructor</u>, <u>check the course syllabus</u>, **or** <u>go to the writing center</u>.*

Choose coordinating conjunctions to complete the following sentences. Add a comma when necessary.

1. Everyone in our class gets along really well _____ preparing for the group presentation was easy.

2. Kaori started to attend free classes at the Writing Center _____ she had received poor grades on her essays in the first semester.

3. Wirat's economics professor is very easy-going during lectures _____ he seems annoyed answering students' questions.

4. Essays can be submitted directly to my office _____ they can be emailed to me as a pdf file.

5. The cost of tuition _____ living arrangements are significant factors when students decide where to attend university.

6. At first, Kyung-Eun had planned to join the tennis club _____ she joined the volunteer society instead.

7. Lin thought his family would distract him from his studies too much _____ he decided to study at a university in another city.

8. To receive a 10% discount, students have to purchase the college's meal vouchers by the month _____ by the semester.

9. Students may not speak during the exam _____ may they use a dictionary.

10. Trang did not study very hard for the exam _____ he got the highest mark in the class.

2. Subordinating conjunctions

When **subordinating conjunctions** begin a clause, the clause becomes dependent. All dependent clauses:

- must be connected to an independent clause in one sentence.
- can be placed **before** or **after** the independent clause.

If the dependent clause is **before** the independent clause, a comma is used:

subordinating conjunction + subject + verb	+ comma +	independent clause

dependent clause

Because parking space is often limited in universities, very few students go to school by car.

Although many smokers know about the risk of smoking, they still cannot break the addiction.

If the dependent clause is **after** the independent clause, a comma is not necessary:

| independent clause | + | **subordinating conjunction** + subject + verb |

dependent clause

*Very few university students in large cities go to school by car **because** parking space on campuses is limited.*

*Many smokers cannot break the addiction **although** they know about the risk of smoking.*

Common subordinating conjunctions include the following:

Relationship between clauses	Subordinating conjunctions
a similar idea	*as*
an opposite or contrasting idea	*although, even though, whereas, while*
a cause or reason	*as, because, since*
a purpose	*so that*
a condition	*if, unless*
a time relationship	*after, as, as soon as, before, since, until, when, while*

Note that some subordinating conjunctions have more than one function:

While *dormitory life involves various constraints, it also brings numerous benefits to students.* (showing an opposite idea)

While *the professor was talking, the students were listening and taking notes.* (showing a time relationship)

See Appendix B (page 120) for a complete list of conjunctions.

Exercise 2   **Circle the best conjunction.**

1. Some students study abroad (even though / because / so that) they are interested in the culture of the country.

2. Studying abroad develops students' language skills, (and / but / so) it gives them an opportunity to live in a different culture.

3. (As / Although / If) people realize the dangers of smoking, the number of non-smokers is increasing.

4. Students who live in a dormitory have to accept many restrictions, (and / but / or) they can learn social skills that might be useful in the future.

5. (Since / If / While) students have much more personal freedom by living alone, they are also responsible for doing all the housework.

6. Social networking sites are interesting and easy to use, (but / or / so) they have rapidly become popular among young people.

7. Many students carry their cell phones all the time (after / so that / unless) they can keep in touch with their friends.

8. (Because / If / Unless) many governments take action to stop global warming, the problem will continue to worsen.

Exercise 3 **Choose one of the following subordinating conjunctions to complete the sentences.**

as, although, since, while, so that, if, whereas, unless

1. _____ most fathers feel obliged to work full-time, not many choose to stay home and raise their children.

2. Students are encouraged to submit their study abroad applications now _____ any problems can be solved before the deadline.

3. Along with his famous Ninth Symphony, many of Beethoven's later piano works were also composed _____ he was deaf.

4. _____ soccer is loved around the world, it is still not popular in many parts of North America.

5. India's population exceeds one billion _____ does China's.

6. _____ the health benefits of drinking tea are widely accepted, the possible benefits of drinking coffee are still being debated.

7. Attending university and working full-time will be difficult _____ the student has high motivation and excellent time-management skills.

8. _____ global warming continues, it could contribute to the mass extinction of many animal species worldwide.

Exercise 4

Join two of the following sentences with a coordinating or subordinating conjunction to make logical sentences. Use commas correctly.

Some teenagers drink under age.

Underage drinking can lead to serious health problems.

The legal drinking age in many countries is between eighteen and twenty-one.

Stores are prohibited from selling alcohol to minors.

Universities should regulate students' drinking more strictly.

Example:

Because underage drinking can lead to serious health problems, stores are prohibited from selling alcohol to minors.

1. _____

_____

2. _____

_____

3. _____

_____

4. _____

_____

5. _____

_____

Transitional expressions are words and phrases that show the last sentence is related to sentences that come before it. They can be categorized into several groups according to their function.

Most transitional expressions are adverbs or adverbial phrases. They are often used at the beginning of a sentence, followed by a comma. Some transitional expressions, however, are noun phrases (adjectives + noun) and are used as a subject.

1. **Listing ideas** *(first, second, finally)*

   First, students whose homes are close enough to school often live with their families. Second, students who live too far away from school to commute might move into a dormitory.

2. **Adding an idea** *(also, another, in addition, moreover)*

   People with university degrees tend to find better-paying jobs than those without them. In addition, some universities provide their students with opportunities to acquire practical skills that can be useful in the real world.

3. **Showing a similar idea** *(like …, likewise, similarly)*

   Students who live with their parents can depend on them for cooking. Similarly, those who live in a dormitory do not have to cook because many dormitories have cafeterias.

4. **Showing an opposite or contrasting idea** *(however, in contrast, on the other hand, unlike …)*

   Students who live with their parents can depend on them to do housework. In contrast, those who live alone have to do all the housework by themselves, even when they are busy.

5. **Showing an effect or result** *(as a result, because of, therefore, thus)*

   People with university degrees tend to find better-paying jobs than those without them. Therefore, many parents wish to send their children to university.

6. **Showing an example** *(for example, for instance)*

   The latest technologies and applications have made communication instant. For example, people who live on opposite sides of the world can be in contact all day through portable devices.

7. **Concluding or summarizing** *(in short, in conclusion, to sum up, to summarize)*

   To sum up, students go to university for a variety of reasons: to study a particular field, to find a good job, or to make friends.

Note that the transitional expressions on the last page are followed by a comma. The following transitional phrases are not followed by a comma:

Another common reason for going to university is that college education often leads to a better career in the future.

The last advantage of working part-time is that students can learn about different occupations through their jobs.

See Appendix C (page 121) for a complete list of transitional expressions.

Exercise 5   **Fill in the blanks with appropriate transitional expressions and commas.**

1. School cafeterias are always crowded, and restaurants outside the campus are expensive. _____ many students bring a lunch from home.

2. Eating fish regularly has numerous health benefits. _____ fatty acids contained in fish reduce the risk of cancer and heart disease. _____ eating fish helps maintain eyesight and makes bones stronger.

3. Small universities can provide students with a friendly atmosphere and personalized care. _____ large schools can offer a wide selection of courses and extra-curricular activities.

4. Tennis is played both individually and in pairs, and requires players to hit a ball over a net. _____ table tennis has singles and doubles and involves players hitting a ball over a net.

5. Many people believe that having eight hours of sleep every day is ideal for maintaining their health. _____ research has found a higher death rate among people who sleep eight hours or longer every day than among people who sleep six or seven hours daily.

6. Backpacking overseas is an interesting and attractive way for students to spend their vacations. It gives them a chance to see the world and experience other cultures. _____ many students enjoy meeting local residents and other travelers.

Section 4   Avoiding run-on sentences and sentence fragments

Run-on sentences and **sentence fragments** are two common types of sentence structure errors. They often occur when a writer misuses a conjunction or transitional expression.

1. Run-on sentences

A **run-on sentence** is made up of two (or more) sentences joined without a conjunction. Sometimes the two sentences have been joined incorrectly with only a comma in between:

✗ *Becoming a university student is an entirely new experience, some people adapt quickly while others struggle to fit in.*

Another common mistake is to join two sentences with a transitional expression. Transitional expressions are not conjunctions; they cannot combine two sentences into one.

✗ *People with university degrees tend to find better-paying jobs than those without them, <u>therefore,</u> many parents wish to send their children to universities.*

To correct a run-on sentence, do one of the following:

- Break it into two separate sentences.
- Use a conjunction.

✓ *Becoming a university student is an entirely new experience. **As a result,** some people adapt quickly while others struggle to fit in.*

✓ ***Because** becoming a university student is an entirely new experience, some people adapt quickly while others struggle to fit in.*

✓ *People with university degrees tend to find better-paying jobs than those without them. **Therefore,** many parents wish to send their children to universities.*

✓ *People with university degrees tend to find better-paying jobs than those without them, **so** many parents wish to send their children to universities.*

2. Sentence fragments

Sentence fragments are incomplete sentences. They are often missing a subject or a verb, or both:

✗ *There are a variety of clubs in most universities. <u>For example,</u> <u>sports teams, drama clubs, and music groups.</u>*

Sentence fragments like the following have a subject and a verb. However, they are not complete sentences because conjunctions are used incorrectly. As you learned in the previous section, conjunctions are words that join two clauses, so do not use a conjunction with only one clause.

✗ Working part-time gives students extra spending money. <u>And helps them learn about society.</u>

✗ Very few students in large cities go to school by car. <u>Because parking space on campuses is limited.</u>

To correct a sentence fragment, do one of the following:

- Make it a complete sentence by adding the missing words.
- Use a transitional expression instead of a conjunction.
- Connect the sentence fragment to a nearby sentence.

✓ *There are a variety of clubs in most universities. For example, sports teams, drama clubs, and music groups can be found in almost every school.*

✓ *There are a variety of clubs in most universities, such as sports teams, drama clubs, and music groups.*

✓ *Working part-time gives students extra spending money. **Moreover, it** helps them learn about society.*

✓ *Working part-time gives students extra spending money, **and it** helps them learn about society.*

✓ *Very few students in large cities go to school by car. **This is** because parking space on campuses is limited.*

✓ *Very few students in large cities go to school by car **because** parking space on campuses is limited.*

Exercise 6

Some of the following sentences are correct, but some are run-on sentences or sentence fragments. Identify these sentences and correct them.

1.   University internship programs are extremely popular because they provide valuable work experience.

2.   Many students use their vacation time to do something they cannot usually do. For example, getting a job, taking a trip, and learning to drive.

3.   By working part-time, students can earn extra money and learn about society. Although working while attending school is sometimes stressful.

4.   One advantage of living alone is that it gives complete freedom to students, another advantage is that students can become independent.

5.   Computers are essential tools in today's education. Even elementary school children are using them.

6.   Email makes communication faster and cheaper, however, it decreases the opportunities for face-to-face communication.

7.   Rent is extremely high in many large cities. So, many students choose to live with their parents.

8.   By studying abroad, students can learn about the culture of another country, and they can gain self-confidence.

Review questions

1.   What is coherence?

2.   What are the differences between coordinating conjunctions and subordinating conjunctions?

3.   What are transitional expressions? Give some examples and their functions.

P a r t

4 Editing a paragraph

The goals of this lesson:

- Recognizing an appropriate style for academic writing
- Editing a paragraph

Section 1 Academic writing style

Academic writing is different from spoken language and personal or informal writing in terms of style. This style should be:
- formal
- objective
- logical

Below is a list of DOs and DON'Ts in academic writing.

To be ...	DOs		DON'Ts	
formal	✓	Use complete, grammatical sentences.	✗	"Talk" to the reader directly, using phrases such as *you should* ... and *why don't you* ... ?
	✓	Use sophisticated vocabulary.	✗	Use colloquial expressions, such as *History lectures are really cool.*
	✓	Use vocabulary that is precise (not vague).	✗	Use contractions, such as *don't* and *can't.*
objective	✓	Write from a third person's point of view.	✗	Use first-person narration, such as *I will discuss* ... and *I will introduce* ...
logical	✓	Organize the writing into paragraphs.	✗	Include irrelevant or unnecessary information.
	✓	Use transitional expressions to show the relationship between sentences.		

Exercise 1

These two paragraphs are written on the same topic. Read them and answer the questions.

1. Which paragraph is more academic, paragraph A or paragraph B?

2. What makes the other paragraph less academic?

Paragraph A

Advantages of Working Part-Time

A part-time job offers many advantages to university students. First, by working in their free time, students can earn extra money. Although most students still have to depend on their parents for tuition and rent, they can use the extra money for buying necessities and going out with friends. In addition, if students have a part-time job, they might be able to develop various skills that they cannot learn in school. For example, students can learn how to communicate appropriately with people of different ages and positions by cooperating with co-workers and serving customers. Certain types of jobs also provide opportunities to acquire technical skills, such as bookkeeping and using computers. Finally, students can learn about different occupations through part-time jobs, and this might help them decide their future career. For instance, by tutoring a child, the student might be able to learn what is required for becoming a teacher. To sum up, part-time jobs give university students not only extra spending money but also many other benefits.

Paragraph B

Advantages of Working Part-Time

I will write about advantages of working part-time. I think working part-time has many advantages for university students. The first advantage is of course money. I work part-time in a restaurant. The money is not enough to pay for school and rent, but I can buy snacks, books, clothes, music and that kind of stuff, and I can go out with my friends too. It's great to have my own money! Second is the skills you can learn. I work at a restaurant. So I have to talk with my boss and senior staff every day. And the customers too. This teaches me how to communicate. Then I have to use a cash register. These kinds of skills are really useful, and I can't learn them in school. Finally, it's good for the future. I don't want to work in a restaurant in the future, so the job is not going to be really useful for me. But it's different with my girlfriend. She wants be a teacher, and her part-time job is a tutor of elementary school kids. I guess she can learn a lot about teaching from that job. My conclusion is, part-time jobs give many wonderful things to university students. I think you should work part-time too. You can get money, plus other great stuff!

Editing is a very important step in the writing process to improve your work. Proper editing requires reading what you have written critically and making necessary changes.

Remember these points about editing:

1. When you edit your writing, you should read your work at least twice.

2. When you read it the first time, check the content and organization by asking yourself questions such as:
    *   Does the topic sentence clearly express the topic and a controlling idea?
    *   Is all the information in the paragraph related to the controlling idea?
    *   Do the supporting points have enough details?

3. When you read the second time, examine each sentence more carefully for correct grammar and style.

During the editing stage, it is useful to ask another student to read your writing. This is called **peer editing**. Peer editing has many benefits. For example, a peer could:
*   find mistakes you missed.
*   tell you if your writing conveys your ideas accurately.
*   suggest improvements.

Section 3   Editing a paragraph

Below is a list of questions to consider when editing your or a peer's writing.

Paragraph Editing Checklist

- **First reading: check for content and organization**

Content

1. Is the paragraph developed with an appropriate amount of information?
2. Do all the supporting points and details support the controlling idea of the paragraph effectively?

Organization

1. Is there a title? Does it represent the topic accurately? Are capital letters used correctly?
2. Does the paragraph have a topic sentence? Does it state the topic and the controlling idea clearly?
3. Are the supporting sentences presented logically?
4. Does the paragraph have a concluding sentence? Does it restate the controlling idea and summarize the supporting points?

- **Second reading: check for grammar and style**

1. Are coordinating conjunctions and subordinating conjunctions used correctly?
2. Are transitional expressions used effectively and accurately?
3. Does the paragraph follow the DOs and DON'Ts of academic writing?

- **Comments**

1. Strengths:

2   Weaknesses:

Edit the paragraph below using the checklist on the previous page. Follow these steps:

1. Read the draft once to check the content and organization.
   - Write some comments (strengths and weaknesses) in the space at the bottom of the checklist.
   - When you comment on a weakness, write a way to improve it.

2. Read the draft again to check for grammatical errors and style problems. Write your corrections on the draft.

Going to University

There are several reasons why students go to university. First, students go to university to make new friends. New friends will give them different ideas and new sense of value. It is interesting to know different ideas, but maybe you can't accept some of them. Another reason for going to university is to study a subject you are interested in more deeply. In high school, you had to study many different subjects. However, in university, you can choose a major and study it deeply. There are many special courses and professors who have a lot of knowledge. So you can learn your major deeply. Finally, students go to university, because they can get a better job in the future. They can learn practical skills which are useful for some jobs through classes and internship program. And people who graduate from university usually get better job than people who don't graduate from university. To sum up, students go to university to make friends, to study subject they are interested in, and to have a good job in the future.

Review questions

1. What are the features of academic writing style?

2. When you edit a draft, how many times should you read it? What should you check first? What should you check later?

3. What is peer editing? Why is it beneficial?

4. What aspects of content and organization should you check when you edit a paragraph?

UNIT 2

Writing an Essay

Part

1 | From a paragraph to an essay

The goals of this lesson:

- Structuring an essay
- Writing a thesis statement
- Writing the topic sentences of body paragraphs
- Making an outline for an essay

Section 1 What is an essay?

An **essay** is a piece of writing that discusses one main topic. It consists of several paragraphs and is divided into three parts:

- introductory paragraph
- body paragraphs
- concluding paragraph

Using this essay structure, writers can focus on several aspects of a topic and explore each one in depth.

Section 2 — The structure of an essay

An essay has the same basic parts as a paragraph. The three major components of an essay (the **introductory paragraph**, the **body paragraphs**, and the **concluding paragraph**) have similar roles to the three components of a paragraph (the topic sentence, the supporting sentences, and the concluding sentence).

Essay

Introductory paragraph

Building sentences

Thesis statement

Body

Body paragraph 1

Topic sentence

Supporting sentences

Concluding sentence

Body paragraph 2

Topic sentence

Supporting sentences

Concluding sentence

Body paragraph 3

Topic sentence

Supporting sentences

Concluding sentence

Concluding paragraph

Restatement of thesis

Summary of body paragraphs

Final thought

Introductory paragraph

- The first paragraph of an essay.
- Consists of two elements:
  1. **Building sentences** – introduce the topic and provide background information about the thesis statement.
  2. **Thesis statement** – presents the **topic, writer's opinion**, and the **main ideas** of the essay.

Body paragraphs

- The main part (the **body**) of the essay.
- Each paragraph develops a main idea in the thesis statement.
- Each paragraph is made up of three parts:
  1. **Topic sentence** – presents the topic and the controlling idea of the paragraph.
  2. **Supporting sentences** – present several points and details that support the controlling idea.
  3. **Concluding sentence** – restates the controlling idea and summarizes the supporting points.

Concluding paragraph

- The last paragraph of an essay.
- Consists of three elements:
  1. **Restatement of the thesis** – presents the thesis statement again using different words.
  2. **Summary of the body paragraphs** – summarizes the main points of the body paragraphs.
  3. **Writer's final thought** – presents the writer's final comment about the essay topic.

Exercise 1   **Read the model essay below.**

1. Identify the three major components: the introductory paragraph, the body paragraphs, and the concluding paragraph.

2. Identify the components of each paragraph (refer to the diagram on page 39).

3. Answer the following questions.

   a. What is the essay topic and the writer's opinion on the topic?

   b. What are the three main ideas?

Reasons for Going to University

At one point or another in their high school lives, students are faced with one big question: should they go to university? Some students decide not to go. They might think that higher education is not necessary for them or that they have something more meaningful to do. Other students decide to go to university. Although these students all think that it is worth spending the next four years in classrooms, the reasons why they think so might be different. Students go to university for a variety of reasons: academic interest, future career, or social life.

First, many students attend university to study a particular subject in depth. University curriculums allow students to choose a major. This is a significant difference from high schools, which require students to take a wide range of classes regardless of their interests. Moreover, universities offer a number of specialized courses in one discipline, and these courses are taught by experts in the fields. Thus, for example, students who are interested in politics can major in political science and take courses about the political system, political philosophy, comparative politics, and other specific topics related to politics. In addition, universities have various research facilities that help students learn, such as libraries, laboratories, and computer rooms. Such curriculums, courses, faculty, and facilities enable students to pursue their academic goals in the field of their choice, and this is one of the reasons why they go to university.

Another common reason for going to university is that a college education often leads to a better career in the future. In many countries, companies tend to look for university graduates to fill positions that have greater responsibility and higher pay, such as managers and supervisors. Furthermore, for certain professions including doctors, lawyers, and school teachers, a university degree is a requirement. In addition, some universities provide students with opportunities to acquire practical skills that can be useful in the real world. For example, they offer courses in accounting, data processing, and foreign languages, as well as internship programs in which students can experience working in a company and learning business skills. In short, some students attend university because a university degree and the practical skills they can acquire will bring them better employment opportunities in the future.

Finally, for some students, making friends and enjoying an active social life can be a sufficient reason to stay in school for another four years. In universities, students have the chance to meet people who come from different places with diverse backgrounds. They might be in the same class with students who work while attending school, older people who returned to school after retirement, or students who come from other countries. In addition, universities have a variety of clubs and student organizations, such as sports teams, hobby groups, and social awareness groups. By joining them, students can spend time with others who have similar interests. Thus, universities can be places to meet a diverse group of people and foster relationships, and these opportunities attract some students to higher education.

In conclusion, students may have different reasons for going to university. For many of them, the main reason is to explore the academic field they are interested in. However, some students attend university to gain an advantage in the job market in the future. Others go to university to meet people with different backgrounds and develop friendships. Regardless of the reason, it is important for students to remember why they are in university and do their best to achieve their goals.

The **thesis statement** is a sentence that appears at the end of the introductory paragraph and is the most important sentence in an essay. The purpose of a thesis statement is to state the writer's opinion on a topic and the reasons why the writer has that opinion.

A thesis statement should have the following elements:
- the **topic** of the essay.
- the **writer's opinion** about the essay topic.
- the **main ideas** supporting the writer's opinion.

Often in an academic essay, the writer's opinion is expressed as a conclusion to a problem or an answer to a question.

Example of an essay question:
What are the reasons for going to university?

Thesis statement:

Essay topic	Writer's opinion	Main ideas

Students go to university _for a variety of reasons_: _academic interest, future career, or social life_.

The thesis statement above is a complete answer to the essay question. With this thesis statement, the essay reader will know:
- the essay topic (reasons for going to university).
- the writer's opinion on the topic (that students go to university for a variety of reasons).
- the main ideas that will be discussed in the body paragraphs to support this opinion (academic interests, future careers and social life).

The thesis statement presents the main ideas in the order they will be discussed in the body paragraphs. In the thesis, the main ideas can be:
- listed after a colon(:), using nouns or noun phrases, as in the example above.
- written without using a colon, as in the thesis statement below.

Essay topic	Writer's opinion

Many students go to university _because university graduates have an advantage in their future career_ _with their degree, specialized knowledge, and practical skills)._

Main ideas

Exercise 2   **Write a thesis statement using the writer's opinion and main ideas below.**

1. **Essay topic:** Clubs at university

   Writer's opinion: There are three types of clubs at university.

   Main ideas:
   1. Sports
   2. Art
   3. Academic

   Thesis statement:

   _____

   _____

2. **Essay topic:** Living in a university dormitory

   Writer's opinion: Living in a dormitory has many benefits for university students.

   Main ideas:
   1. They can make friends.
   2. They can learn social skills.
   3. They can save money.

   Thesis statement:

   _____

   _____

3. **Essay topic:** Academic writing skills for university students

   Writer's opinion: Academic writing skills are important for university students for several reasons.

   Main ideas:
   1. Help students complete university assignments successfully.
   2. Lead to good grades.
   3. Help students in their future careers.

   Thesis statement:

   _____

   _____

A topic sentence is the first sentence of each body paragraph. Effective topic sentences show the reader how the body paragraphs support the thesis statement of the essay.

Topic sentences have two parts:

Part 1: The **topic** and the **writer's opinion** on the topic.

Part 2: The **controlling idea**, which comes from one of the main ideas presented in the thesis statement.

In Part 1, the topic and writer's opinion should be expressed in the topic sentences to keep the reader focused on what the essay is about. Compare the thesis statement and topic sentences from the model essay on page 41:

Thesis statement:

Students go to university for a variety of reasons: academic interest, future career, or social life.

Body paragraph 1 topic sentence:

First, many students attend university to study a particular subject in depth.

Body paragraph 2 topic sentence:

Another common reason for going to university is that a college education often leads to a better career in the future.

Body paragraph 3 topic sentence:

Finally, for some students, making friends and enjoying an active social life can be a sufficient reason to stay in school for another four years.

In Part 2, however, the controlling idea will be different in each topic sentence, since each paragraph will focus on developing only one of the main ideas from the thesis statement. The controlling idea tells the reader which main idea from the thesis statement will be developed in a particular body paragraph. Compare the thesis statement and topic sentences from the model essay on page 41.

Thesis statement:

Students go to university for a variety of reasons: academic interest, future career, or social life.

Body paragraph 1 topic sentence:

First, many students attend university to study a particular subject in depth.

Body paragraph 2 topic sentence:

Another common reason for going to university is that a college education often leads to a better career in the future.

Body paragraph 3 topic sentence:

Finally, for some students, making friends and enjoying an active social life can be a sufficient reason to stay in school for another four years.

After the topic sentence, all the information in a body paragraph must only support the controlling idea.

Note: To avoid confusing the reader, present the body paragraphs in the same order as the main ideas are presented in the thesis statement.

Exercise 3

The following are alternative topic sentences for each body paragraph in the model essay. Identify the problem with each topic sentence and write it in the space provided.

Thesis statement:
Students go to university for a variety of reasons: academic interest, future career, or social life.

Body paragraph 1 topic sentence:
First, students can study a particular subject in depth.

Problem:

_____

_____

Body paragraph 2 topic sentence:
Second, there is another common reason why students go to university.

Problem:

_____

_____

Body paragraph 3 topic sentence:
Finally, I will talk about one more reason.

Problem:

_____

_____

Transitional expressions for listing ideas (e.g., *first, second, another idea, finally*) are often used in the topic sentence to indicate both the order of the main ideas, and to indicate the beginning of a new paragraph.

In the model essay, the body paragraphs are in the same order as the main ideas in the thesis statement, and they begin with transitional words.

Thesis statement:
Students go to university for a variety of reasons: **academic interest (A), future career (B), or social life (C)**.

Body paragraph 1 topic sentence:
(First,)many students attend university to **study a particular subject in depth**.

Body paragraph 2 topic sentence:
(Another common reason)for going to university is that a college education often leads to **a better career in the future**.

Body paragraph 3 topic sentence:
(Finally,) for some students, **making friends and enjoying an active social life** *can be a sufficient reason to stay in school for another four years.*

C

Avoiding repetition in topic sentences

Topic sentences need to include the topic and opinion in the thesis statement. However, to avoid repetition, write each topic sentence using different words from the thesis. In the model essay, the topic and opinion in the thesis statement are expressed in the topic sentences using different words, but their meaning is the same each time.

Thesis statement:
(Students go to university for a variety of reasons:)academic interest, future career, or social life.

Body paragraph 1 topic sentence:
First,(many students attend university to)study a particular subject in depth.

Body paragraph 2 topic sentence:
Another common(reason for going to university)is that a college education often leads to a better career in the future.

Body paragraph 3 topic sentence:
Finally, for some students, making friends and enjoying an active social life can be a sufficient(reason to stay in school for another four years.)

Exercise 4

Rewrite the following topic sentences so that they include the topic of the essay and the writer's opinion.

Essay topic: Living in a university dormitory
Writer's opinion: Living in a university dormitory has many benefits for university students.

Body paragraph 1 topic sentence:
First, students can make friends.

_____

_____

Body paragraph 2 topic sentence:
Second, students can learn social skills.

_____

_____

Body paragraph 3 topic sentence:
Finally, students can save money.

_____

_____

Exercise 5

Read the following information and write a topic sentence for each body paragraph.

1. **Essay topic:** Clubs at university

    Writer's opinion: There are three types of clubs at university.

    Main ideas:
    1. Sports
    2. Art
    3. Academic

    Body paragraph 1 topic sentence:

    _____

    _____

    Body paragraph 2 topic sentence:

    _____

    _____

    Body paragraph 3 topic sentence:

    _____

    _____

2. **Essay topic:** Academic writing skills for university students

   Writer's opinion: Academic writing skills are important for university students for several reasons.

   Main ideas:
   1. Help students complete university assignments successfully.
   2. Lead to good grades.
   3. Give students an advantage in their future career.

   Body paragraph 1 topic sentence:

   _____

   _____

   Body paragraph 2 topic sentence:

   _____

   _____

   Body paragraph 3 topic sentence:

   _____

   _____

Section 6   Making an essay outline

After writing a thesis statement and topic sentences, the next step is to choose **supporting points** for each body paragraph. As you learned in Unit 1, these points must provide examples and reasons that support the controlling idea of that paragraph.

Once you have chosen supporting points, put all the ideas in an **outline**. An outline for an essay should include the following:
- topic of the essay.
- thesis statement (in a complete sentence).
- topic sentence of each body paragraph (in a complete sentence).
- supporting points in each body paragraph.

Exercise 6   **Using the form below, complete an outline of the model essay on page 41.**

OUTLINE

Topic: Reasons for going to university

Thesis statement:
Students go to university for a variety of reasons: academic interest, future career, or social life.

Body paragraph 1
Topic sentence:
First, many students attend university to study a particular subject in depth.

Supporting points:

1. Students can choose a major.

2. Many specialized courses taught by experts.

3. _____

Body paragraph 2
Topic sentence:
Another common reason for going to university is that a college education often leads to a better career in the future.

Supporting points:

1. Companies hire university graduates to fill positions with greater responsibility and higher pay.

2. _____

3. _____

Body paragraph 3
Topic sentence:
Finally, for some students, making friends and enjoying an active social life can be a sufficient reason to stay in school for another four years.

Supporting points:

1. _____

2. _____

Choose one of these essay topics and write the outline of a five-paragraph essay. Use the outline on the next page.

1. Reasons for studying abroad

2. Advantages of joining a university student organization

3. Causes of stress among university students

4. Factors in choosing a university

5. Ways technology can help university students

Follow these steps:

Step 1 Brainstorm ideas.

Step 2 Form an opinion.

Step 3 Choose three main ideas.

Step 4 Write a thesis statement.

Step 5 Write a topic sentence for each body paragraph.

Step 6 Choose supporting points for each body paragraph.

OUTLINE

Topic: _____

Thesis statement:

_____

_____

Body paragraph 1
Topic sentence:

_____

_____

Supporting points:

_____

_____

Body paragraph 2
Topic sentence:

_____

_____

Supporting points:

_____

_____

Body paragraph 3
Topic sentence:

_____

_____

Supporting points:

_____

_____

Review questions

1. What are the three major components of an essay?
2. What are the elements of the thesis statement?
3. What information should you include in the topic sentence of a body paragraph?
4. What should you include in an essay outline?

Part
2 | Writing an essay

The goals of this lesson:

- Developing body paragraphs
- Writing an introductory paragraph
- Writing a concluding paragraph

Developing body paragraphs

In an essay, the topic is divided into main ideas, and an entire paragraph is used to discuss each main idea. In order to write a body paragraph of a reasonable length, you have to develop the main idea by providing enough details to support it. For example, the first body paragraph of the model essay about reasons for going to university (page 41) gives three supporting points and provides details for each one.

Supporting point 1

Details

Supporting point 2

Details

Supporting point 3

Details

First, many students attend university to study a particular subject in depth. University curriculums allow students to choose a major. This is a significant difference from high schools, which require students to take a wide range of classes regardless of their interests. Moreover, universities offer a number of specialized courses in one discipline, and these courses are taught by experts in the fields. Thus, for example, students who are interested in politics can major in political science and take courses about the political system, political philosophy, comparative politics, and other specific topics related to politics. In addition, universities have various research facilities that help students learn, such as libraries, laboratories, and computer rooms. Such curriculums, courses, faculty, and facilities enable students to pursue their academic goals in the field of their choice, and this is one of the reasons why they go to university.

Exercise 1   This is an outline of the model essay on page 41. Read the essay again and write down the details used in body paragraphs 2 and 3.

OUTLINE

Topic: Reasons for going to university

Thesis statement:
Students go to university for a variety of reasons: academic interest, future career, or social life.

Body paragraph 1
Topic sentence:
First, many students attend university to study a particular subject in depth.

Supporting points:
1. Students can choose a major.
    High school students have to take a wide range of subjects.

2. Many specialized courses taught by experts.
    Political science – political system, political philosophy, comparative politics.

3. Various research facilities.
    Libraries, laboratories, computer rooms.

Body paragraph 2
Topic sentence:
Another common reason for going to university is that a college education often leads to a better career in the future.

Supporting points:
1. Companies hire university graduates to fill positions that have greater responsibility and higher pay.

2. Certain professions require a university degree.

    _____

3. Universities provide opportunities to acquire practical skills.

    _____

Body paragraph 3
Topic sentence:
Finally, for some students, making friends and enjoying an active social life can be a sufficient reason for staying in school for another four years.

Supporting points:
1. Students can meet a diverse group of people.

    _____

2. Students can join a student organization.

    _____

Look at the outline below. Brainstorm details for each supporting point and add them to the outline.

OUTLINE

Topic: Living situations of university students

Thesis statement:
Living situations of university students can be classified into three types: living with their families, living in a dormitory, and living alone in an apartment.

<u>**Body paragraph 1**</u>
Topic sentence:
First, students whose homes are close enough to school often live with their families.

Supporting points:
1. Students can depend on their families to do housework.

   _____

2. Some students feel uncomfortable.

   _____

<u>**Body paragraph 2**</u>
Topic sentence:
Second, students who live too far away from school to commute might move into a dormitory.

Supporting points:
1. Involves various constraints.

   _____

2. Students can learn social skills.

   _____

<u>**Body paragraph 3**</u>
Topic sentence:
Finally, living alone in an apartment is a popular choice among students who cannot commute to school from their homes but do not like the inconveniences of dormitory life.

Supporting points:
1. Students can be free from rules and restrictions.

   _____

2. Students have to be independent and responsible.

   _____

Section 2   Writing an introductory paragraph

The **introductory paragraph** of an essay consists of two components:

- **building sentences**
- a **thesis statement**

Building sentences introduce the essay topic and provide background information so that the reader can better understand the essay topic. The thesis statement then presents the writer's specific opinion about the topic and main ideas of the essay.

A common technique for writing an introductory paragraph is to organize the information from **general** to **specific**. The paragraph:

- begins with a general fact about the essay topic.
- then presents more specific information sentence-by-sentence that leads to the thesis statement at the end of the paragraph.

Read this introductory paragraph of the model essay about reasons for going to university.

Building sentences

At one point or another in their high school lives, students are faced with one big question: should they go to university? Some students decide not to go. They might think that higher education is not necessary for them or that they have something more meaningful to do. Other students decide to go to university. Although these students all think that it is worth spending the next four years in classrooms, the reasons why they think so might

Thesis statement

be different. Students go to university for a variety of reasons: academic interest, future career, or social life.

The focus of the paragraph becomes increasingly specific, as shown in the diagram on the next page.

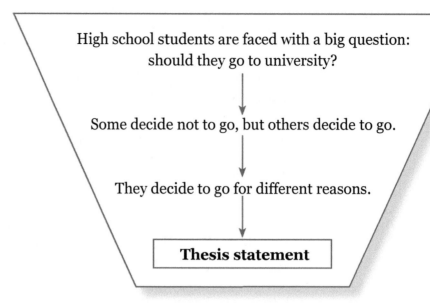

High school students are faced with a big question: should they go to university?

↓

Some decide not to go, but others decide to go.

↓

They decide to go for different reasons.

↓

Thesis statement

When writing an introductory paragraph, be careful not to make the opening sentence too general. If it is too general, it will be difficult to link its meaning to the thesis statement. Compare the following introductory paragraph with the one on the previous page.

Building sentences {

The average life expectancy of people is over 80 years in some countries. During this long life span, people make many important decisions. They decide where to live, what to do for a living, whether to get married, and whether to have children. For many people, one of the earliest decisions they have to make happens when they are in high school because they have to decide whether to go to university. Some students decide not to go. They might think that higher education is not necessary for them or that they have something more meaningful to do. Other students decide to go to university. Although these students all think that it is worth spending the next four years in classrooms, the reasons why they think so might

Thesis statement

be different. Students go to university for a variety of reasons: academic interest, future career, or social life.

The opening sentence of this introductory paragraph is too general because life expectancy is not related to reasons for going to university. As a result, the paragraph became unnecessarily long with extra information in the building sentences.

To write an effective opening sentence, think about possible themes related to the thesis. For example, in the first thesis statement, the essay writer considered two themes:

- making a decision
- education

Thesis:

Theme 1: making a decision

Students go to university for a variety of reasons: academic interest, future career, or social life.

Theme 2: education

These themes were used to help write the opening sentence of the introductory paragraph.

Opening sentence:

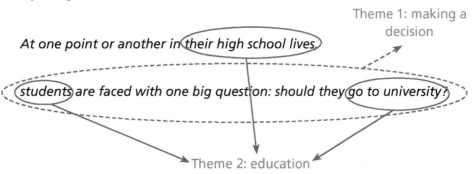

Theme 1: making a decision

At one point or another in their high school lives, students are faced with one big question: should they go to university?

Theme 2: education

Finding possible themes in the thesis helps you write a more focused opening sentence, and makes the building sentences more concise.

Reorder the sentences to make an effective introductory paragraph for an essay. Make sure that sentences are ordered from general to specific, and that the paragraph ends with the thesis statement.

1. Topic: Types of clubs at university

   a. These students often join clubs to meet people who have the same hobbies or interests.

   b. Covering such a wide range of interests, university clubs can be categorized into three major types: sports, arts, and academic.

   c. It is not difficult to find a group to join as most universities have numerous student organizations featuring a variety of activities.

   d. For many students, universities are not only places for studying; they are places for making friends and enjoying their hobbies.

   e. Students who like soccer can join a soccer team, those who play musical instruments can join an orchestra, and those who are interested in journalism can be an editor of the school newspaper.

2. Topic: Advantages of working part-time for university students

   a. Although working while attending school is sometimes stressful, many students still get a job, because it brings a number of benefits they cannot obtain in classrooms.

   b. Students work after class or on weekends in a variety of places.

   c. By working part-time, university students can earn extra money, develop various skills, and learn about different occupations.

   d. Others work outside the schools as waiters, salespersons, office assistants, or tutors.

   e. These days it is unusual to find university students who have never had a part-time job.

   f. Some work on campus, assisting professors or helping in the library or cafeteria.

Exercise 4

Write the building sentences for an introductory paragraph which connect to the thesis statement.

1. Topic: Causes of stress among university students

_____

_____

_____

_____

_____

_____

_____

_____

_____

_____

Thesis:
Common causes of stress among university students can be classified into three types: assignment deadlines, grades, and job hunting.

2. Topic: Factors in choosing a university

_____

_____

_____

_____

_____

_____

_____

_____

_____

Thesis:
Majors, location, and tuition are three factors which many students consider when they choose a university.

The concluding paragraph consists of three components:
- restatement of the thesis.
- summary of the body paragraphs.
- the writer's final thought.

1. Restatement of the thesis

The first sentence of the concluding paragraph is a restatement of the topic and opinion from the thesis statement. To restate these parts of the thesis statement, use a different sentence structure and different words when possible.

Compare the thesis statement of the model essay with the restatement of the thesis:

Students go to university for a variety of reasons: academic interest, future career, or social life.

Restatement of the thesis:

In conclusion, _students may have different reasons for attending university_.

Thesis restatements often begin with one of the following transitional expressions to indicate the start of the concluding paragraph:

In conclusion,
To conclude,
To summarize,   } _... students may have different reasons for going to university._
To sum up,
In short,

2. Restatement of the main ideas

The sentences after the restated thesis are restatements of the topic sentences. If it is a five-paragraph essay with three body paragraphs, you should write three sentences to restate each topic sentence. Use a different sentence structure and different words when possible to restate each topic sentence.

Below are the topic sentences of the body paragraphs in the model essay on page 41. Compare them with the restatements of the topic sentences.

Body paragraph 1 topic sentence:
First, many students attend university to study a particular subject in depth.

Body paragraph 2 topic sentence:
Another common reason for going to university is that a college education often leads to a better career in the future.

Body paragraph 3 topic sentence:

Finally, for some students, making friends and enjoying an active social life can be a sufficient reason to stay in school for another four years.

Topic sentence 1

Restatements of the topic sentences:

For many of them, the main reason is to explore the academic field they are interested in. However, some students attend university to have an advantage in the job market in the future. Others go to university to meet people with different backgrounds and develop friendships.

Topic sentence 2

Topic sentence 3

Exercise 5

Write restatements for the following thesis statements and topic sentences.

1. **Thesis statement:**

   Living situations of university students can be classified into three types: living with their families, living in a dormitory, and living alone in an apartment.

   Body paragraph 1 topic sentence:

   First, students whose homes are close enough to school often live with their families.

   Body paragraph 2 topic sentence:

   Second, students who live too far away from school to commute might move into a dormitory.

   Body paragraph 3 topic sentence:

   Finally, living alone in an apartment is a popular choice among students who cannot commute to school from their homes but do not like the inconveniences of dormitory life.

   Restatement of the thesis:

   _____

   _____

   _____

   Restatements of the topic sentences:

   _____

   _____

   _____

   _____

   _____

   _____

   _____

   _____

2. **Thesis statement:**
Living in a university dormitory is beneficial because students can make friends, learn social skills, and save money.

Body paragraph 1 topic sentence:
One benefit of living in a university dormitory is that students can make friends easily.

Body paragraph 2 topic sentence:
Another valuable benefit of living in a university dormitory is that students can learn social skills.

Body paragraph 3 topic sentence:
Finally, saving money is a significant advantage of living in a university dormitory.

Restatement of the thesis:

_____

_____

_____

Restatements of the topic sentences:

_____

_____

_____

_____

_____

_____

_____

_____

_____

3. **Thesis statement:**

By working part-time, university students can earn extra money, develop various skills, and learn about different occupations.

Body paragraph 1 topic sentence:

One advantage of working part-time for university students is that they can have money to spend on themselves.

Body paragraph 2 topic sentence:

Furthermore, by working part-time, students can learn a variety of skills that will be useful in the future.

Body paragraph 3 topic sentence:

The last advantage of working part-time is that students can gain first-hand knowledge about various occupations.

Restatement of the thesis:

_____

_____

_____

Restatements of the topic sentences:

_____

_____

_____

_____

_____

_____

_____

_____

_____

3. The final thought

The last sentence of the concluding paragraph expresses the writer's overall opinion or prediction about the essay topic. The purpose of this sentence is to:

- leave the readers with a strong impression.
- encourage the readers to think about the topic after they finish reading the essay.

Read the last sentence of the model essay:

Regardless of the reason, it is important for students to remember why they are in university and do their best to achieve their goals.

This sentence expresses the writer's **overall opinion** about the topic. This is one way to leave an impression and encourage readers to think about the topic further.

Another type of effective final thought states a **prediction** for the future. For example, the final thought of the model essay could be:

Whether academic or non-academic, having a clear reason for going to school will help students make the best of the four years they will spend on campus.

When writing a final thought:

- **Do not** use *I* or *you*. Write from a third person's point of view.
- **Do not** introduce any new ideas or details. The final thought must be relevant to what has already been presented in the essay.

Compare the following final thoughts:

✓ *Regardless of the reason, it is important for students to remember why they are in university and do their best to achieve their goals.*

✗ *I think that it is important for students to remember why they are in university and do their best to achieve their goals.* (use of *I*)

✗ *Regardless of the reason, you should remember why you are in university and do your best to achieve your goals.* (use of *you*)

✗ *In reality, however, many students go to university for no particular reason and spend the four years without accomplishing anything.* (introduces an idea not mentioned in the essay)

Exercise 6   The following final thoughts are for the essays described in Exercise 5 (pages 61–63). Rewrite them to make them more appropriate.

1. **Topic:** Living situations of university students

    Final thought: Because these three living situations have both advantages and disadvantages, you should consider your needs and desires carefully and choose the most suitable one.

    Rewrite:

    _____

    _____

    _____

2. **Topic:** Living in a university dormitory

    Final thought: I think I will remember my two years in a dormitory as my best university experience.

    Rewrite:

    _____

    _____

    _____

3. **Topic:** Advantages of working part-time for university students

    Final thought: However, the most important responsibility of students is to study, so they should not spend too much time working.

    Rewrite:

    _____

    _____

    _____

Review questions

1. How should you organize the sentences in the introductory paragraph?
2. What are the three components of the concluding paragraph? What order do they come in?
3. What should you avoid when you write your final thought?

Part

3 | Editing an essay

The goals of this lesson:

- Using pronouns
- Editing an essay

Section 1 Using pronouns

Using pronouns effectively creates better style because:
- it allows writers to refer to topics in previous sentences without repeating the same words.
- it improves coherence by showing the connections between sentences clearly.

The following text demonstrates how pronouns are used.

> First, many students attend university to study a particular subject in depth. <u>University curriculums allow students to choose a major</u>. (This) is a significant difference from high schools, which require <u>students</u> to take a wide range of classes regardless of (their) interests. Moreover, universities <u>offer a number of specialized courses</u> in one discipline, and (these) courses are taught by experts in the fields. Thus, for example, students who are interested in politics can major in political science and take courses about the political system, political philosophy, comparative politics, and other specific topics related to politics. In addition, universities have research facilities that help students learn, such as libraries, laboratories, and computer rooms. <u>Such curriculums, courses faculty, and facilities enable students to pursue (their) academic goals in the field of their choice</u>, and (this) is one of the reasons why (they) go to university.

As seen in Unit 1, Part 4, academic writing should be written from a third person's point of view. This means that as a writer, you discuss the topic as an outsider, and the reader also reads your essay as an outsider. Diagram A below illustrates the appropriate relationship between the writer, the topic, and the reader in academic writing. Compare it with Diagrams B, C, and D, in which the writer, the reader, or both see the topic as his or her own issue.

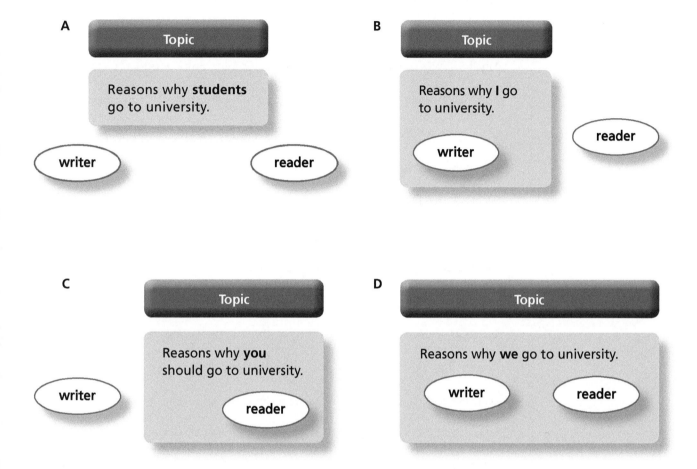

To write in the third person:

- Use the third person pronouns (*he* or *she*, *they*, *one*).
- Avoid the first person pronouns (*I*, *we*) or second person pronouns (*you*). Using the third person all the time will help achieve coherence and objectivity.

Read the following paragraph and then do the task.

1. Replace some of the pronouns with ones more appropriate for academic writing.

2. Replace nouns with pronouns wherever appropriate.

———————————————————◆————————————————————

Finally, living alone in an apartment is a choice among students who cannot
                                          their
commute to school from ~~students'~~ homes but do not like the inconveniences of
                                     students   *their*
dormitory life. In this living situation, ~~we~~ can be free from ~~our~~ parents as well as

the rules and restrictions of dormitory life. We can stay up as late as we want, eat

whatever we like, and invite our friends to our place anytime. However, students

are required to be independent and responsible in this living situation. As students'

parents do not watch the students and take care of the students, it is all up to

the students to lead a healthy and orderly life. You have to do all the housework

by yourself even when you are busy with your study. You have to manage your

own budget so that you can save enough money for the rent, utilities, and other

bills. In short, students who want freedom often choose to live by themselves in

apartments, but students need to be mature enough to take care of themselves in

this living situation.

———————————————————◆————————————————————

Section 2   Editing an essay

Editing an academic essay requires careful review of the **content**, **organization**, and **language** (grammar and style) to ensure the ideas are presented clearly and logically.

Below is a list of questions to ask when editing a draft. Use the same questions when peer editing.

Essay Editing Checklist

- **First reading: check the essay for content and organization.**

Content

1. Is any information not relevant to the thesis statement?
2. Are the body paragraphs developed with appropriate amounts of details?
3. Do the details support the main ideas effectively?

Organization

1. Does the essay have three basic components: an introductory paragraph, body paragraphs, and a concluding paragraph?

Introductory paragraph

2. Are building sentences ordered from general to specific?
3. Is there a clear thesis statement at the end of the paragraph? Does it state the topic, writer's opinion, and the main ideas?

Body paragraphs

4. Does the topic sentence clearly state the controlling idea of the paragraph?
5. Are the supporting sentences presented logically?

Concluding paragraph

6. Does the paragraph begin with an effectively restated thesis?
7. Does the paragraph effectively restate the topic sentences from the body paragraphs?
8. Is the writer's final thought presented at the end? Is it relevant to the essay topic?

- **Second reading: check the essay for grammar and style.**

1. Are conjunctions used correctly?
2. Are transitional expressions used effectively?
3. Are pronouns used correctly?
4. Is the style of writing appropriate for an academic essay?

Edit the essay below using the checklist on the previous page. Follow these steps:

1. Read the draft once to check the content and organization. Write some comments (strengths and weaknesses) on a separate sheet of paper. When you comment on a weakness, suggest a way to improve it.

2. Read the draft again to check for grammatical errors and style problems. Write your corrections on the draft.

Advantages of Working Part-Time for University Students

Nowadays, it is difficult to find university students who have never worked any part-time job. Working part-time has many advantages for university students. By working part-time, students can make extra money, develop various skills, and learn about different occupations.

First, by working part-time, students can have money that they can use freely. This is especially important for students who live alone because they have to pay for apartment, electricity, water, food, and so on by themselves. Money from part-time job is maybe not enough for paying all of these, but students can help their parents. Moreover, for students who don't live alone, it is important to have extra money. Because they need money for club activities, playing with friends, and buying favorite things. In short, one of the advantages of working part-time is, students can have extra money.

Second, students can learn various skills. Almost part-time jobs require workers to communicate with people every day. For example, if student works in a restaurant, student has to greet customers and answer customers' questions politely. In addition, student has to communicate with his or her boss and coworkers to work smoothly. In addition, some part-time jobs teach students practical skills. For example, answering telephone, using cash register, and using computer. Like this, students can learn skills that students cannot learn in university.

Finally, students can learn about different jobs. Nowadays, job hunting is very severe. We should start preparing for it early. By working different part-time jobs, we can learn about good things and bad things of different jobs. To sum up, students can learn about various occupations by working part-time.

In conclusion, working part-time has many advantages for university students. It might be hard to work while going to school, but you should experience it at least once while you are in university.

Review questions

1. Why is it important to use pronouns effectively?
2. What aspects of content and organization should you check when you edit an essay?

Paraphrasing, Summarizing and Citing Information

1 | Paraphrasing and summarizing

The goals of this lesson:

- Paraphrasing
- Summarizing

Section 1 | Introduction

In all academic writing, using information from outside sources like books, articles, magazines and the internet is essential. Writers use this information to support their opinion. There are three basic ways to add information from outside sources into academic writing: **quoting**, **paraphrasing**, and **summarizing**.

Quoting information involves taking the same words from the source, putting quotation marks at the beginning and end of these words, and then adding this to your writing. Quoting will be introduced in more detail in the next part (Unit 4, Part 2, pages 109–110).

A more common way to use outside source information is by **paraphrasing** and **summarizing**. This involves rewriting sentences in different words. They are essential skills because in academic writing you need to:

- use information from outside sources, but write this information in your own words and style.
- restate the content of the essay – e.g., thesis statement or topic sentences – in the concluding paragraph without repeating the same words.

The table on the next page describes similarities and differences between paraphrasing and summarizing.

Paraphrasing	Summarizing
• Change the sentence structure of the original text. • Change the vocabulary of the original text.	
• Use all the details in the original text. • A paraphrase is often a similar length as the original.	• Use only the most important ideas in the original text. • A summary is significantly shorter than the original.

Section 2   Paraphrasing

A paraphrase must be written in your own words and structure. However, it must contain the same details as the original. Therefore, when paraphrasing:

• do not change any of the ideas in the original information.

• do not remove any ideas, or add new ones.

It is not necessary to change every word in the original information when you paraphrase. In fact, certain kinds of words and phrases should not be changed because they cannot be stated in any other way. These words and phrases are called **shared language**. Examples of shared language include:

• proper nouns (names of people, organizations, places, etc.):

 Albert Einstein   the European Union   Cambridge University   Singapore

• common nouns that are difficult to reword efficiently:

 history   computer   mosquito   summer   technology

• technical terms:

 carbon dioxide   hibernation   gross national product

• numbers and dates:

 17,000   42%   1987   October 22

Compare the following paraphrases of this original sentence:

Only 9% of the students who work part-time earn sufficient income to support themselves.

Alternative paraphrases:

✗ a. *Only 9% of the students who have part-time jobs make enough money to support themselves.*

✗ b. *Although many students work part-time, only 9% of them make their living from their jobs because their wages are very low.*

✓ c. *Of all the students who have part-time jobs, no more than 9% make enough money to earn a living.*

Paraphrase **a** is not a good paraphrase. It keeps the details in the original sentence, but the sentence structure and vocabulary are too similar to the original. **Paraphrase b** is also inappropriate because it includes information that is not in the original text. **Paraphrase c** is the best paraphrase. It conveys the details in the original text accurately and uses a different structure and vocabulary.

Exercise 1 **Choose the best paraphrase of the original text. Explain your answer.**

1. Due to the shortage of space, on-campus housing is not common in big city universities. Most students commute from their home or rent an apartment near the campus.

   Paraphrases:

   a. In large cities, the number of university students living on campus is small because schools often lack space for dormitories. Most students live with their families or live in apartments near their schools.

   b. Because of the shortage of space, on-campus housing is rare in big city universities. Most students go to school from their home or live in an apartment nearby.

   c. In big cities, not so many university students live on campus. It is more common for them to live with their parents or live alone in an apartment near the school.

2. Throughout most of the developed world, universities have seen a steady increase in the number of women enrolling in engineering courses.

   Paraphrases:

   a. There are increasingly more engineering schools in most of the developed areas of the world because women are now taking the courses they offer.

   b. The percentage of women studying engineering at university has been rising steadily in a majority of developed countries.

   c. In most developed countries, universities reported a consistent increase in the number of women taking engineering courses.

Unit 3 • Part 1

How to paraphrase

To paraphrase, follow this five-step process.

Step 1 Read the original text. Make sure you understand it:

Only 9% of the students who work part-time earn sufficient income to support themselves.

Step 2 Identify and write down:

- the shared language *(9%, students).*
- details from the original using different words *(part-time jobs, make enough money, earn a living).*

Step 3 Using only the words and phrases in your notes, write your paraphrase. **Do not look at the original text.**

First draft →

Of all the students who work part-time jobs, 9% make enough money to earn a living.

Step 4 Compare your paraphrase with the original. Check the following:

- Does the paraphrase have the same meaning as the original?
- Does the paraphrase use different sentence structure and vocabulary from the original sentence?
- As a general rule, if you have taken more than three words in a row from the original sentence, you should rewrite that part.

Step 5 Revise your paraphrase as necessary:

Final paraphrase →

Of all the students who <u>have</u> part-time jobs, <u>just</u> 9% make enough money to earn a living.

Exercise 2

Paraphrase these sentences following the steps described above.

1. Due to the widespread availability of imported food, even ordinary people's diets are becoming internationalized.

   _____

   _____

   _____

2. Medical officials blame sedentary activities like internet use and video games for the dramatic jump in obesity among teenagers.

   _____

   _____

   _____

3. Children who have pets while they are growing up are more likely to be calmer when they are adults.

_____

_____

_____

4. Tablet computers will not only make textbooks obsolete, but also potentially revolutionize education.

_____

_____

_____

5. Australian research found that athletes who did warm-up activities before doing exercise had just as many injuries as those who did no warm-up.

_____

_____

_____

Section 3   Summarizing

Summarizing is similar to paraphrasing because it involves rewriting the original text using different vocabulary and structure. However, a summary is different in that it:
- only has the main idea from the original text.
- is much shorter than the original text.

> The number of overweight children is predicted to rise significantly around the world by the end of the decade. Research conducted in 25 countries has concluded that almost every country showed significant increases in childhood obesity. Almost 50% of children in the U.S., Canada and Latin America will be overweight by 2020; in China, this figure is estimated to be one in five. Scientists believe this will mean that health care services will be seriously affected in the future. Many obese children will become obese adults, which will result in many of them suffering from heart disease, stroke, and other weight-related ailments.

Compare these summaries of the original passage on the previous page.

✗ a. A survey in 25 countries has found out that the number of obese children will increase significantly all over the world by 2020. Scientists agree that this will influence health care services in the near future because many overweight children will suffer from weight-related problems when they become adults.

✗ b. Since the number of overweight children will increase around the world, health care services will be seriously affected in the future.

✓ c. The increasing number of obese children around the world will cause serious problems to medical services.

Summary a is too long and too specific. It captures the main idea of the original passage but includes many unnecessary details. **Summary b** is too similar to the original in sentence structure and vocabulary choice. **Summary c** is the best. It expresses the main idea of the original passage, and the vocabulary and sentence structure are different from the original.

Exercise 3

Choose the best summary of the original passage. Explain your answer.

> The need for sophisticated equipment is not the only obstacle limiting the use of modern medical science. Traditional medicine, which uses a wide variety of inexpensive, easily accessible, and familiar natural ingredients and techniques, is preferable for many people. Medicines are normally created from local plants, animals, and minerals. Techniques often include socially bonding physical contact between patient and healer like rubbing or massaging, and spiritual experiences which may involve trances, music, and scents. In Africa, for instance, an estimated 80% of people rely on traditional medicine for almost all their health care. Similarly, in many other parts of the world, particularly in Asia and Latin America where modern facilities are available, this approach to medicine is highly valued because it is effective, inexpensive, and culturally significant.

Summaries:

a. Because of its effectiveness, low cost, and cultural value, many people in the world prefer traditional medicine to modern medicine.

b. Many people around the world use traditional medicine because they cannot afford expensive modern medicine.

c. In Africa, Asia, and Latin America, traditional medicine is considered better than modern medical science because traditional medicines and techniques use inexpensive, easily accessible, and familiar natural ingredients, and involve physical contact between the doctor and the patient such as rubbing and massaging.

How to summarize

To summarize, follow this six-step process.

Step 1 Read the original passage. Make sure you understand it.

Step 2 Identify the key point or points. These are supported by specific details, statistics, and examples.

Key point {

The number of overweight children is predicted to rise significantly around the world by the end of the decade. Research conducted in 25 countries has concluded that almost every country showed significant increases in childhood obesity. Almost 50% of children in the U.S., Canada and Latin America will be overweight by 2020; in China, this figure is estimated to be one in five. Scientists believe this will mean that

} Support for key point

Key point {

health care services will be seriously affected in the future. Many obese children will become obese adults, which will result in many of them suffering from heart disease, stroke, and other weight-related ailments.

} Support for key point

Step 3 From the key points, identify and write down:
- the shared language (*obese, children*).
- details from the original using different words (*increase, cause problems, medical services*).

Step 4 Using only the words and phrases in your notes, write your summary. **Do not look at the original text**.

First draft ⟶ *The increasing number of obese children will cause problems to medical services.*

Step 5   Compare your summary with the original text. Check the following:

- Does the summary use different vocabulary?
- Does the summary have a different sentence structure?
- Does the summary include only key points? (The summary should not include specific details, statistics, or examples.)
- Does the summary avoid using more than three words in a row from the original?

Step 6   Revise your summary as necessary.

Final summary

The increasing number of obese children <u>worldwide</u> will cause <u>serious</u> problems to medical services.

Exercise 4

Summarize these passages in one sentence.

1.

Slow Food is an international movement that aims to preserve local food cultures and make people aware of the benefits of a traditional diet. It was launched in Italy in the late 1980s with the establishment of the first local association and now is supported by more than 800 local groups in over 50 countries. The movement has several missions. One of them is to protect the gastronomic culture and traditional foods in each area. This mission comes from a concern that diversity in diet might disappear as fast food becomes a standard item on people's tables all over the world. Another goal of the Slow Food movement is to make healthy, safe foods available to everyone. For this purpose, the foundation rewards small-scale farmers who supply such products to their communities. Finally, Slow Food advocates are committed to informing citizens, especially young ones, about their regional food cultures and teaching them how to enjoy the taste of traditional dishes. To achieve this goal, local groups hold "taste education" workshops and seminars in their areas.

_____

_____

_____

2. Since 1970, the number of allergy sufferers around the world has risen dramatically. The current estimate of people with some kind of allergy is an astounding 30 to 40%. The direct causes of the increase are unclear, but most researchers attribute the growing figure to a combination of environmental and social changes resulting from the effects of rapid post-war industrialization, modernization and globalization. Increased industrial pollution, crowded cities, small, poorly ventilated apartments with air conditioning and new synthetic building materials, dietary changes, more cosmetics and modern medicine are all blamed as the main contributors. Paradoxically, over-cleanliness has also been identified as a cause. Some researchers claim the widespread use of home cleaning agents and their resulting germ-free environments have weakened children's immune systems and created vulnerable adults. Perhaps most striking, however, is the growing number of food allergies. Modern global trade has allowed foods formerly unknown to people to become easily accessible. This has resulted in more allergic reactions due to the increase in opportunities for people to eat new foods their bodies have never encountered before.

Review questions

1. How are paraphrasing and summarizing similar? How are they different?
2. How do you paraphrase? Describe the steps.
3. How do you summarize? Describe the steps.

2 Citing the sources of information

The goals of this lesson:

- Making in-text citation
- Making a Works Cited list

Introduction

When using outside sources in your essay, include information which identifies each source: the author's name, title of the book or article, and other details about the source. This is called **citing** or **citation**.

By citing the sources, you show:

- that these ideas or words are not yours.
- where these ideas or words in your essay came from and who created these ideas or words.
- where readers can find the source so they can check or learn more about the information.

Citing source information also prevents **plagiarism**. "Plagiarism" means using another person's words or ideas and presenting them as your own. It is a form of theft because it is stealing another person's ideas. Committing plagiarism can result in serious consequences, such as your essay being rejected or even failing your course. In order to avoid plagiarism, it is important to:

- present the words or ideas in the appropriate style (paraphrases, summaries or quotations).
- cite the source using the correct format.

Most information from sources that is used in your essay needs to be cited. However, there are a few situations where information does not need to be cited. If the information is **common knowledge**, you do not have to identify the source. Common knowledge includes the following:

1   A fact that is widely known and accepted as a truth:

   The blue whale is the largest mammal on earth.

   The population of the world today is estimated to be 6.5 billion.

2   An event that was widely reported:

   In December 2004, an undersea earthquake occurred off the coast of Sumatra causing enormous tsunamis and killing over 200,000 people in South and Southeast Asia.

NOTE: If you are unsure whether information is common knowledge, then it is always best to cite it.

Citation has two parts:

•   **in-text citation**.

•   a **Works Cited list**.

Both must be included in your essay.

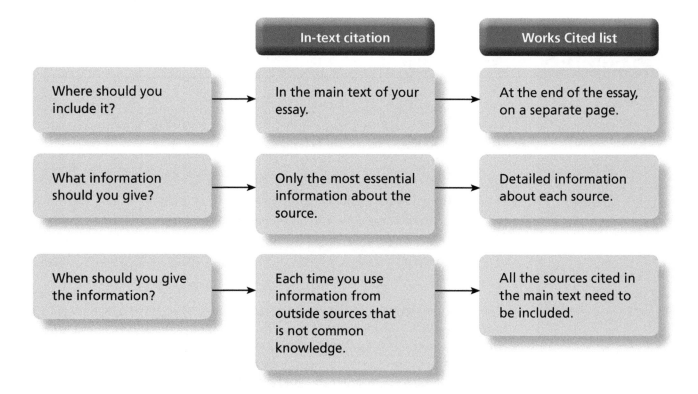

	In-text citation	Works Cited list
Where should you include it?	In the main text of your essay.	At the end of the essay, on a separate page.
What information should you give?	Only the most essential information about the source.	Detailed information about each source.
When should you give the information?	Each time you use information from outside sources that is not common knowledge.	All the sources cited in the main text need to be included.

Section 2   Making in-text citation (MLA format)

The purpose of in-text citation is to give just enough information so the reader can easily find the source in the Works Cited list, but not interfere with the flow of your writing.

The fundamental rules of in-text citation, according to the Modern Language Association (MLA) are:

- Always give the last name of the author of the source.
- Always give the page number or numbers of the source of the information.
- When the author's name is not available, give the title of the source.

Following these rules, the specific format of in-text citation varies according to the type of source used:

1. **You have the author's name and the page number.**

   a. Include the author's last name at the beginning of the paraphrase, summary or quotation using a **reporting word** (see page 85). Give the page number in parentheses at the end:

   Dickinson reports that the number of students entering university level education throughout Asia has been steadily rising for the last 15 years (12).

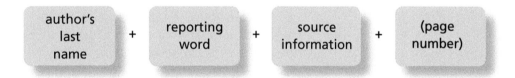

   b. Give the author's name and the page number in parentheses at the end of the paraphrase, summary or quotation:

   The number of students entering university level education throughout Asia has been steadily rising for the last 15 years (Dickinson 12).

2. **You have the author's name but not the page number.**

   Give the author's name at the beginning of the paraphrase, summary or quotation using a reporting word:

   Stumpel argues that if the amount of garbage in the oceans continues to grow, several species of sea birds will soon experience devastating population declines.

3. **You do not have the author's name.**

   Write down the title of the source in parentheses at the end of the paraphrase, summary or quotation:

   Ecotourism now accounts for an estimated 30% of tourism revenues in the tropical regions of Central and South America ("A Different Tiger Economy" 8–9).

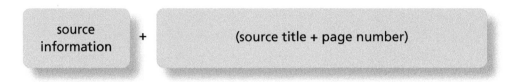

   - *Italicize* or <u>underline</u> the title of a book, journal, magazine, newspaper or website name.
   - Use quotation marks around the title of an article from a book, journal, magazine, newspaper or website (see also Appendix A on page 119).
   - When the title is long, give only the first few words.
   - If the page number is available, write it down after the title.

4. **Information from a secondary source.**

   Sometimes information you find in a source already has in-text citation. The following is a sentence from a magazine article written by a biologist named Lars Heskey:

   In 1978 the Australian government conducted a national survey on the kangaroo population and concluded that kangaroo numbers increased due to the widespread implementation of European farming methods.

   The sentence says that the information comes from a survey by the Australian government. It means that this magazine article can only be a **secondary source** of the information.

   When you use a secondary source:
   - Include the name of the original source author in the paraphrase, summary or quotation.
   - Give the name of the secondary source author in parentheses at the end of the paraphrase, summary or quotation. Put the phrase **qtd. in** before the name.
   - If the page number is available, give it after the author's name in the parentheses.
   - In the Works Cited list, give the information of the secondary source only.

   *A survey by **the Australian government** in 1978 found that a significant factor in the continuing prevalence of the kangaroo population throughout Australia was the introduction of European farming methods **(qtd. in Heskey 75)**.*

   It is always better to use the original source (the survey by the Australian government) and cite that source in your essay, if possible. If you do this, you do not have to use Heskey's article.

5. Reporting words.

In academic essays, a variety of reporting words are used to identify the author of the information from outside sources. By using these words, you can integrate paraphrases, summaries and quotations into your essay. Common reporting words include the following:

(author)	*says / said that*	(paraphrase)
	states / stated that	
	reports / reported that	
	argues / argued that	
	claims / claimed that	

According to   (author)

Examples:

Valente reports that *Puerto Madryn, a coastal city in Argentina, attracted only 17,000 whale watchers in 1991, but the number leaped to more than 100,000 by 2006.*

According to Ellis, *the Inupiat people in Alaska go out to sea in small boats and kill whales with old hand-thrown harpoons.*

Exercise 1

Using the source information given, make in-text citation to the following paraphrases, summaries, or quotations. (You do not have to use all the information given.)

1. Garbage left behind around Mount Everest by past climbers now poses a serious threat to the environment and a hazard to other climbers.

   Source:

Author:	Jeremy Rivers
Title of article:	"A Mount Everest Makeover"
Title of newspaper:	The Vancouver Globe
Date of publication:	December 2, 2005
Edition:	late edition, section 1
Page:	4

2. Major environmental problems caused by tourism include the depletion of natural resources, pollution, and various physical damages caused by construction and tourist activities.

   Source:

Author:	United Nations Environment Programme
Title of book:	Environmental Impacts of Tourism
City of publication:	Nairobi
Publisher:	United Nations Environment Programme
Year:	2003
Pages:	5–6

3. UCLA biologist Pat Farber said, "It is a failure of imagination that we humans cannot see value in animals beyond their use to us as food or entertainment."

   Source:

Author:	John Convertino
Title of article:	"How We See Animals, How We See Ourselves"
Title of magazine:	Perspectives on Nature
Date of publication:	May 2005
Page of quotation:	27

4. Every year, an estimated 25 million vertebrate animals are used for the purpose of research, experiment and education in the U.S.

   Source:

Author:	(not given)
Article title:	"Frequently Asked Questions about Animals in Research"
Title of website:	Animals in Research
Name of organization associated with the website:	The Humane Society of the United States
Date of access:	December 8, 2006
URL:	http://www.hsus.org/animals_in_research.htm

5. According to a United Nations report, approximately 25% of the mammals and 12% of the birds in the world might become extinct during the next few decades due to global warming.

   Secondary source:

Author:	Roberta Schultz
Article title:	"An Endangered Planet"
Title of on-line newspaper:	Ocean Tern News
Date of publication:	February 15, 2004
Date of access:	March 5, 2007
URL:	http://www.oceanternnews.com/environment/report/0529.htm

Section 3 — Making a Works Cited list (MLA Format)

In addition to making in-text citation, every research essay must have a **Works Cited list**. The Works Cited list must be on a separate page at the end of the essay. The sources must be ordered alphabetically according to the first letter of the first word. For each source, you have to give full details, including the author's name, title and publication information, in a fixed order. The information you must include varies slightly according to the type of source. Refer to the following MLA formats:

1 A book

Author's Last Name, Author's First Name. *Title of Book*. City of Publication: Publisher, Year.

Example:
Scruton, Roger. *Animal Rights and Wrongs*. London: Demos, 1996.

2 An article in a magazine

Author's Last Name, Author's First Name. "Title of Article." *Title of Magazine* Date of publication: Page number(s) of the entire article.

Example:
Benson, Neill. "Citizen Cetacean." *Pelagem Mammalia* Apr. 2010: 87–90.

3 An article in a newspaper

Author's Last Name, Author's First Name. "Title of Article." *Title of Newspaper* Date of publication, edition: Page number.

Example:
Ellis, Mark. "Living in the Arctic." *London Herald* 25 Nov. 2006, late ed.: B5.

4 An article in an online newspaper

Author's Last Name, Author's First Name. "Title of Article." *Title of Online Newspaper* Date of publication. Date of access <URL>.

Example:
Shukman, David. "Hunting Minke with the Norwegeans." *BBC News Online* 9 May 2005. Accessed 17 Jan. 2007 <http://news.bbc.co.uk/2/hi/science/nature/4530415.stm>.

5 An article on a website

Author's Last Name, Author's First Name. "Title of Article." *Title of Website*. Date of publication or latest update (if given). Name of Organization Associated with the Website (if any). Date of access <URL>.

Example:
Fezner, Kyoko. "Oceans Under Threat." *Sea Vigil*. 28 Aug. 2006. Sea Vigil Foundation. Accessed 14 Dec. 2006 <http://www.seavigilfoundation.org/en/SEA_NEWS/pastarts/2467-f8be5.htm>.

If the source is written by **two or more authors**, list all the names in the order they appear on the title page. Reverse the order of names only with the first author:

Gunter, Barrie, and Adrian Furnham. *Pets and People: The Psychology of Pet Ownership*. London: Whurr Publishers, 1999.

If the author's **name is not given**, begin with the title:

"Whaling." *Fact Sheets*. Marine Mammal Protection Society. Accessed 26 Jan. 2007 <http://www.protectmarinemammals.org/factsheets/whaling/28271.htm>.

If the source is written by **a group**, use the name of the group as the author:

World Society for the Protection of Animals. *Troubled Waters: A Review of the Welfare Implications of Modern Whaling Activities*. London: World Society for the Protection of Animals, 2004.

When you have created a Works Cited list, check if the information in the list matches the information in the in-text citation:

- Does the Works Cited list include all the sources cited in the essay?
- Does each entry in the Works Cited list begin with the name or title given in the in-text citation?

The following example shows how in-text citation refers to the Works Cited.

First, whaling should be banned because it is morally unacceptable to kill intelligent mammals brutally. Although the method of catching and killing whales has changed greatly over the years, it still remains cruel and ineffective. According to the World Society for the Protection of Animals, whales today are killed by explosive harpoons, which enter the whale near the head and explode inside its body. However, this method is far from effective as shown by the fact that only about 40% of the whales harpooned die immediately (2). In addition, these hunting methods go against modern society's acceptable standard of animal suffering. Benson found that "people surveyed around the world now correctly understand that whales are intelligent, social mammals, not fish, and if hunted, must receive instant, painless death" (88). Commercial whalers have shown that they cannot meet this international ethical standard, and thus this practice must stop.

Works Cited

Benson, Neill. "Citizen Cetacean." *Pelagem Mammalia* **Apr. 2010: 87–90.**

Darby, Andrew. *Harpoon: Into the Heart of Whaling*. New York: De Capo Press, 2008.

Holt, Sidney. "Counting Whales in the North Atlantic." *Science* Jan. 2004: 39–55

Valente, Marcela. "Latin America Unites to Defend Whales." *IPS* 4 Dec. 2006. Accessed 6 Jan. 2007 <http://ipsnews.net/news.asp?idnews=35711>.

"Whaling." *Fact Sheets*. Marine Mammal Protection Society. Accessed 9 Jan. 2007 <http://www.savemammal.org/factsheets/whaling/28271.htm>.

World Society for the Protection of Animals. *Troubled Waters: A Review of the Welfare Implications of Modern Whaling Activities*. **London: World Society for the Protection of Animals, 2004.**

Another reason why commercial whaling needs to cease is that it is no longer economically sustainable. First, whale meat is no longer a popular food even in countries that hunt whales commercially. Whale meat from past hunts is frozen and stored in warehouses, often for many years because consumer demand is so low ("Whaling"). This demonstrates a shift in modern eating habits. Eating whale is simply no longer considered desirable or necessary, and thus the shrinking market for it does not justify the amount of meat produced. This also results in governments subsidizing many whalers to keep them in business. With the meat supply far exceeding demand, Darby reports that the price of whale meat has dropped nearly 80% in some places (344). Many commercial whalers, therefore, rely on government money because the income earned from whaling is insufficient to make a living. In short, meat from commercial whaling no longer has a market, and whalers actually cost taxpayers considerable money by requiring government funds to cover their operating losses.

Works Cited

Benson, Neill. "Citizen Cetacean." *Pelagem Mammalia* Apr. 2010: 87–90.

Darby, Andrew. *Harpoon: Into the Heart of Whaling*. New York: De Capo Press, 2008.

Holt, Sidney. "Counting Whales in the North Atlantic." *Science* Jan. 2004: 39–55

Valente, Marcela. "Latin America Unites to Defend Whales." *IPS* 4 Dec. 2006. Accessed 6 Jan. 2007 <http://ipsnews.net/news.asp?idnews=35711>.

"Whaling." *Fact Sheets*. Marine Mammal Protection Society. Accessed 9 Jan. 2007 <http://www.savemammal.org/factsheets/whaling/28271.htm>.

World Society for the Protection of Animals. *Troubled Waters: A Review of the Welfare Implications of Modern Whaling Activities*. London: World Society for the Protection of Animals, 2004.

Finally, commercial whaling is no longer necessary because other business opportunities offer much better financial rewards. Today, ecotourism is a booming industry, and whale watching can be an important source of income for areas with large numbers of whales. For this reason, many developing countries, such as Argentina, Brazil and South Africa have banned whaling in their oceans and have promoted the development of whale watching industries (Holt 48). This has helped increase the number of visitors to these countries, and as a result, has brought profits to many local communities. For example, Valente reports that Puerto Madryn, a coastal city in Argentina, attracted only 17,000 whale watchers in 1991 but the number leaped to more than 100,000 by 2006. Thus, even if commercial hunting were banned, whaling countries could survive or even flourish more than before by promoting whale watching.

Works Cited

Benson, Neill. "Citizen Cetacean." *Pelagem Mammalia* Apr. 2010: 87–90.

Darby, Andrew. *Harpoon: Into the Heart of Whaling*. New York: De Capo Press, 2008.

Holt, Sidney. "Counting Whales in the North Atlantic." *Science* Jan. 2004: 39–55.

Valente, Marcela. "Latin America Unites to Defend Whales." *IPS* 4 Dec. 2006. Accessed 6 Jan. 2007 <http://ipsnews.net/ news.asp?idnews=35711>.

"Whaling." *Fact Sheets*. Marine Mammal Protection Society. Accessed 9 Jan. 2007 <http://www.savemammal.org/factsheets/whaling/28271.htm>.

World Society for the Protection of Animals. *Troubled Waters: A Review of the Welfare Implications of Modern Whaling Activities*. London: World Society for the Protection of Animals, 2004.

The following are sentences from a research essay and the Works Cited list from the same essay. Find four errors with the in-text citations.

1. It is reported that the value of the exotic pet industry has risen over 30% during the last five years to a massive $7.8 billion ("A Taste for the Exotic").

2. For example, according to the *Cascadia Fish and Wildlife Council,* many species of lizards, snakes, rodents, and turtles carry salmonella bacteria.

3. Edward states that when exotic animals kept as pets escape or are released by their owners, many survive and establish breeding populations in their new environment. These new foreign species often damage or destroy the native animal and plant species ("The Threat of Invasive Spercies").

Works Cited

Cascadia Fish and Wildlife Council. *The Risks of Keeping Exotic Pets.* Portland: Cascadia Ministry of Environment, 2003.

Nichols, Edward. "The Threat of Invasive Species." *New York Chronicle* 14 Mar. 2003, late ed.: F2.

Rodriguez, Anna. "A Taste for the Exotic." *Urban Castle Online.* 7 Nov. 1998. <http://www.urbancastleonline.net/domestic/features/TE1180034.html>.

Create a Works Cited list for the five sources in Exercise 1 (pages 85–86). Use the information given.

Review questions

1. What are the two types of citation you have to include in an essay? How are they different?

2. What information should you give in in-text citation?

3. In what order should you arrange the entries of a Works Cited list?

UNIT
4

Writing a
Research Essay

1 Developing and organizing a research essay

The goals of this lesson:

*   Identifying the structure of a research essay
*   Generating ideas for a research essay
*   Writing a thesis statement for a research essay
*   Writing topic sentences for a research essay
*   Making an outline for a research essay

Section 1 | What is a research essay?

In a research essay, the writer takes a **position** on a topic and uses outside sources to support this position. Many positions on a topic are possible, so you must present arguments to support the position you have taken. In an academic research essay, these **arguments** are based on facts and details gathered from research to convince the reader that what you are saying is correct. If you do not include facts and details from outside sources to support your ideas, the essay will be considered a subjective personal opinion and will not be strong enough to convince the reader.

The steps in writing a research essay are as follows. The writer:

1. is presented with or chooses a topic.
2. researches the topic to understand the various positions.
3. takes a position on the topic.
4. presents arguments using facts and details which were researched to persuade the reader to accept that position.

All outside sources presented in the essay, such as paraphrases, summaries and quotations must be properly cited if they are not common knowledge (see page 82).

Section 2 The structure of a research essay

Like other types of essays, a research essay consists of three parts: the introductory paragraph, the body paragraphs, and the concluding paragraph. The diagram below shows a common pattern of organization for a five-paragraph research essay.

Research essay

Introductory paragraph

Building sentences

Thesis statement
(writer's position)

Body

**Body paragraph 1
(Argument 1)**

Topic sentence

Supporting sentences

Concluding sentence

**Body paragraph 2
(Argument 2)**

Topic sentence

Supporting sentences

Concluding sentence

**Body paragraph 3
(Argument 3)**

Topic sentence

Supporting sentences

Concluding sentence

Concluding paragraph

Restatement of thesis

Summary of body paragraphs

Final thought

Introductory paragraph

Consists of two elements:
1. **Building sentences** introduce the topic and give background information about the topic.
2. The **thesis statement** presents the essay topic, the writer's position, and the main ideas supporting the position.

Body paragraphs (supporting paragraphs)

Each body paragraph uses one of the main ideas from the thesis to make an argument supporting the writer's position. Each paragraph has the following parts:
1. The **topic sentence** introduces the first main idea supporting the position in the thesis.
2. **Supporting sentences** present supporting points and provide details.
3. The **concluding sentence** restates the main idea and summarizes the supporting points.

Concluding paragraph

Consists of three elements:
1. The **restatement of the thesis** states the writer's position again using different words.
2. The **summary of the body paragraphs** summarizes the main ideas of each body paragraph.
3. The **final thought** presents the writer's feeling or prediction about the essay topic.

Exercise 1

1. Read the sample essay on the next page and identify the components of each paragraph described above.

2. Answer the following questions.

   a. What is the writer's position on this issue?
   b. What are the writer's three arguments?

Topic: Should whaling be banned?

No Reason for Commercial Whaling

Since humans first built boats and fished the seas, they have hunted whales. This practice remains culturally significant for many small communities around the world who hunt a few whales each year using traditional methods. In contrast, for other people, whaling has become a high-tech industry using sophisticated equipment to hunt and kill thousands of whales each year for profit. Although these whalers also cite cultural tradition to justify their annual hunts, commercial whaling is strongly opposed by an increasing number of people worldwide. Indeed, the practice of killing whales on an industrial scale is now internationally seen as morally wrong and economically unsound. Therefore, commercial whaling should be banned because it causes excessive suffering to intelligent mammals, is no longer economically viable, and can be replaced by economically beneficial whale watching.

First, whaling should be banned because it is morally unacceptable to kill intelligent mammals brutally. Although the method of catching and killing whales has changed greatly over the years, it still remains cruel and ineffective. According to the World Society for the Protection of Animals, whales today are killed by explosive harpoons, which enter the whale near the head and explode inside its body. However, this method is far from effective, as shown by the fact that only about 40% of the whales harpooned die immediately (2). In addition, these hunting methods go against modern society's acceptable standard of animal suffering. Benson found that "people surveyed around the world now correctly understand that whales are intelligent, social mammals, not fish, and if hunted, must receive instant, painless death" (88). Commercial whalers have shown that they cannot meet this international ethical standard, and thus this practice must stop.

Another reason why commercial whaling needs to cease is that it is no longer economically sustainable. First, whale meat is no longer a popular food, even in countries that hunt whales commercially. Whale meat from past hunts is frozen and stored in warehouses, often for many years because consumer demand is so low ("Whaling"). This demonstrates a shift in modern eating habits. Eating whale is simply no longer considered desirable or necessary, and thus the shrinking market for it does not justify the amount of meat produced. This also results in governments subsidizing many whalers to keep them in business. With the meat supply far exceeding demand, Darby reports that the price of whale meat has dropped nearly 80% in some places (344). Many commercial whalers, therefore, rely on government money because the income earned from whaling is insufficient to make a living. In short, meat from commercial whaling no longer has a market, and whalers actually cost taxpayers considerable money by requiring government funds to cover their operating losses.

Finally, commercial whaling is no longer necessary because other business opportunities offer much better financial rewards. Today, ecotourism is a booming industry, and whale watching can be an important source of income for areas with large numbers of whales. For this reason, many developing countries, such as Argentina, Brazil and South Africa have banned whaling in their oceans and have promoted the development of whale watching industries (Holt 48). This has helped increase the number of visitors to these countries, and as a result, has brought profits to many local communities. For example, Valente reports that Puerto Madryn, a coastal city in Argentina, attracted only 17,000 whale watchers in 1991, but the number leaped to more than 100,000 by 2006. Thus, even if commercial hunting were banned, whaling countries could survive or even flourish more than before by promoting whale watching.

In conclusion, as the evidence shows, whaling is cruel and economically unnecessary and therefore should be prohibited. The current method of killing whales causes intelligent mammals to suffer unnecessarily. Furthermore, because whale meat is no longer a significant part of people's diets, its price has fallen causing the industry to rely on public money. Finally, commercial whaling countries have no reason to continue hunting, as whale watching is an economically more preferable option. Whaling has a long history and has played an important role in the past. However, social values and tastes have changed, and with change, some traditions adapt and survive while others cannot, and die. For commercial whaling, the latter seems inevitable and preferable.

Works Cited

Benson, Neill. "Citizen Cetacean." *Pelagem Mammalia* Apr. 2010: 87–90.

Darby, Andrew. *Harpoon: Into the Heart of Whaling.* New York: De Capo Press, 2008.

Holt, Sidney. "Counting Whales in the North Atlantic." *Science* Jan. 2004: 39–55

Valente, Marcela. "Latin America Unites to Defend Whales." *IPS* 4 Dec. 2006. Accessed 16 Jan. 2007 <http://ipsnews.net/news asp?idnews=35711>.

"Whaling." *Fact Sheets.* Marine Mammal Protection Society. Accessed 26 Jan. 2007 <http://www.protectmarinemammals.org/factsheets/whaling/28271.htm>.

World Society for the Protection of Animals. *Troubled Waters: A Review of the Welfare Implications of Modern Whaling Activities.* London: World Society for the Protection of Animals, 2004.

Section 3   Beginning a research essay

Before writing a research essay, you should read and list the different views on the topic. Be sure to indicate from which outside source the information came. Use the author's name, the title of the publication, or the article name, and the page number.

For example, below is a list made from research on the topic "Should commercial whaling be banned?" From the list, you can then decide which position on the topic (for or against) you will take in your essay and choose the three strongest main ideas that will support this position.

Should commercial whaling be banned?	
Arguments **FOR** the ban	Arguments **AGAINST** the ban
• Whales are very intelligent animals. It is unethical to kill them for food. (World Society for the Protection of Animals) • Whales are killed by cruel methods. They have to suffer from pain before dying. (Tiaoqui pg 380) • The style of commercial whaling today is different from traditional whaling. (Benson pg 88) • Whale meat is rarely eaten nowadays. (Whaling Myths) • People do not have to eat whale meat because there are many other sources of food. (Valente) • People in whaling towns can survive by protecting whales and promoting whale watching. (Holt pg 48)	• It is natural for humans to kill animals for food, and whales should be treated in the same way as other animals. (European Whaling Investigation Team) • The methods of whaling have been improved and made more humane. (Guo pg 12) • In some countries and regions, whaling is a traditional activity that has lasted for hundreds of years. (Whale Population Report) • In some cultures, whale meat is an important part of diet. (Harker) • If whaling were banned, whalers would lose their jobs, and whaling communities would disappear. (Scientific Whaling) • Fish stocks can be maintained by controlling the number of whales. (Dang pg 721)

Tip: Note the source of each idea in parenthesis so you know who to cite if you use these ideas in your essay.

Choose one of the topics below and list ideas for and against it. Decide your position, and give two or three main ideas to support it.

1. Are zoos necessary?

2. Should people be allowed to kill animals for their fur?

3. Should people be allowed to keep animals as pets?

4. Should people be allowed to drive their cars in downtown areas?

5. Do the benefits of tourism outweigh its costs?

Section 4   Writing a thesis statement for a research essay

The thesis statement of a research essay should state:
*   the essay topic.
*   the writer's position.
*   the main ideas supporting the position that will be discussed in the body paragraphs.

In a research essay, the main ideas are the writer's three main arguments (reasons for having that position). The following thesis statement states the writer's position on whaling and announces the three main ideas to be argued in the body paragraphs:

essay topic and writer's position

Therefore, <u>commercial whaling should be banned</u> because <u>it causes excessive suffering to intelligent mammals</u>, <u>is no longer economically viable</u>, <u>and can be replaced by economically beneficial whale watching</u>.

main ideas = writer's arguments

Writer's position: Commercial whaling should be banned.

Arguments (main ideas):
1. Unacceptable pain to whales
2. No longer profitable
3. Economically less preferable than whale watching

When you write a thesis statement for a research essay, you can also list the main ideas first and then state your position, as in this example:

main ideas = writer's arguments

Therefore, <u>because it causes excessive suffering to intelligent mammals</u>, <u>is no longer economically viable</u>, <u>and can be replaced by economically beneficial whale watching</u>; <u>commercial whaling should be banned</u>.

writer's position

Exercise 3

Write thesis statements using the information below.

1. **Position:** People should stop using animals for entertainment.

   Arguments:
   1. It makes animals suffer physically and mentally.
   2. Events using animals can be replaced by other forms of entertainment.
   3. It encourages a disrespectful attitude towards other forms of life.

   Thesis statement:

   _____

   _____

   _____

   _____

2. **Position:** Owning exotic pets like parrots and monkeys should be banned.

   Arguments:
   1. They are dangerous wild animals.
   2. Many are endangered species.
   3. People cannot care for them properly.

   Thesis statement:

   _____

   _____

   _____

   _____

3. **Position:** Animal experiments should be banned.

   Arguments:
   1. It is unethical to harm animals this way.
   2. Alternative methods are just as effective.
   3. The benefits gained by animal testing are minor.

   Thesis statement:

   _____

   _____

   _____

   _____

The body paragraphs present the arguments supporting the writer's position. Therefore, when you write the topic sentences of body paragraphs, you should do the following:

- Use a transitional expression for listing (e.g., *first*, *second*).
- Include the position from the thesis.
- State the argument (one of the main ideas from the thesis).

For an example of this, review the topic sentences in the body paragraphs of the sample essay on page 95:

Body paragraph 1, topic sentence:

writer's position   Argument 1

First, *whaling should be banned* because *it is morally unacceptable to kill intelligent mammals brutally*.

Body paragraph 2, topic sentence:

writer's position

Another reason why *commercial whaling needs to cease* is that *it is no longer economically sustainable*.

Argument 2

Body paragraph 3, topic sentence:

writer's position

Finally, *commercial whaling is no longer necessary* *because other business opportunities offer much better financial rewards*.

Argument 3

Exercise 4   **Write a topic sentence for each body paragraph using the ideas below.**

1. **Position:** People should stop using animals for entertainment.

   Arguments:
   1. It makes animals suffer physically and mentally.
   2. Events using animals can be replaced by other forms of entertainment.
   3. It encourages a disrespectful attitude towards other forms of life.

   Body paragraph 1, topic sentence:

   _____

   _____

   _____

   Body paragraph 2, topic sentence:

   _____

   _____

   _____

   Body paragraph 3, topic sentence:

   _____

   _____

   _____

2. **Position:** Owning exotic pets like parrots and monkeys should be banned.

   Arguments:
   1. They are dangerous wild animals.
   2. Many are endangered species.
   3. People cannot care for them properly.

   Body paragraph 1, topic sentence:

   _____

   _____

   _____

   Body paragraph 2, topic sentence:

   _____

   _____

   _____

   Body paragraph 3, topic sentence:

   _____

   _____

   _____

3. **Position:** Animal experiments should be banned.

   Arguments:
   1. It is unethical to harm animals this way.
   2. Alternative methods are just as effective.
   3. The benefits gained by animal testing are minor.

   Body paragraph 1, topic sentence:

   _____

   _____

   _____

   Body paragraph 2, topic sentence:

   _____

   _____

   _____

   Body paragraph 3, topic sentence:

   _____

   _____

   _____

Section 6 Making an outline for a research essay

An outline for a research essay should include the following:
- the topic of the essay.
- the thesis statement (in a complete sentence).
- the supporting argument (main idea) of each body paragraph.
- the topic sentence of each body paragraph (in a complete sentence).
- supporting points in each body paragraph.

Exercise 5   **Use the form on the next page to complete an outline for the sample essay on page 95.**

OUTLINE

Topic: Should commercial whaling be banned?

Thesis statement:

Therefore, commercial whaling should be banned because it causes excessive suffering to intelligent mammals, is no longer economically viable, and can be replaced by economically beneficial whale watching.

Body paragraph 1

Topic sentence:

First, whaling should be banned because it is morally unacceptable to kill intelligent mammals brutally.

Supporting points:

1. _____

2. _____

Body paragraph 2

Topic sentence:

Another reason why commercial whaling needs to cease is that it is no longer economically sustainable.

Supporting points:

1. _____

2. _____

Body paragraph 3

Topic sentence:

Finally, commercial whaling is no longer necessary because other business opportunities offer much better financial rewards.

Supporting points:

1. _____

2. _____

Exercise 6

Look at the notes you made in Exercise 2. Using some of those ideas, and the outline form on the next page, create an outline for a five-paragraph research essay. Follow these steps:

Step 1 Research the topic.

Step 2 Decide your position on the topic and choose supporting arguments.

Step 3 Write a thesis statement.

Step 4 Write a topic sentence for each body paragraph.

Step 5 Write the supporting points for each body paragraph.

OUTLINE

Topic: _____

Thesis statement:

_____

_____

Body paragraph 1
Topic sentence:

_____

_____

Supporting points:

_____

_____

Body paragraph 2
Topic sentence:

_____

_____

Supporting points:

_____

_____

Body paragraph 3
Topic sentence:

_____

_____

Supporting points:

_____

_____

Review questions

1. What is the purpose of a research essay?

2. What kind of information should you try to find when doing research?

3. What information should you include in the thesis statement of a research essay?

4. What information should you include in the topic sentence of each body paragraph?

2 | Supporting arguments

The goals of this lesson:

- Supporting arguments with outside sources
- Presenting information from outside sources

Supporting arguments with outside sources

The purpose of a research essay is to persuade the reader to accept the writer's position. Therefore, it is crucial for the writer to make strong arguments. To make strong arguments in a research essay, support your arguments with specific information found in outside sources such as books, academic journals, magazines, newspapers, and internet sites.

Through research, you will find different types of information which can provide support for your arguments. Types of information include:

1. Facts (things accepted as truths):

   Tigers are the largest of all cat species, and can be found from the Siberian taiga to the tropical mangrove swamps of South Asia.

2. Anecdotes (incidents or other people's experiences):

   In the first half of 2008, tigers killed seven fishermen in a coastal area of India called Netidhopani.

3. Statistics (figures based on a survey):

   There were an estimated 40,000 tigers in India last century. In 2002, their population was 3,642, and in 2008 it had shrunk to 1,411.

4. Experts' opinions:

   According to Pradip Guha of the World Conservation Union, endangered tigers are attacking humans as rising sea levels and coastal erosion gradually reduces their natural habitat.

Section 2   Organizing supporting sentences

In this first body paragraph of the model essay about whaling, three pieces of information from outside sources are used to explain the writer's two supporting points.

Supporting point 1

Information 1 (fact)

Information 2 (statistics)

Supporting point 2

Information 3 (expert's opinion)

First, whaling should be banned because it is morally unacceptable to kill intelligent mammals brutally. Although the method of catching and killing whales has changed greatly over the years, it still remains cruel and ineffective. According to the World Society for the Protection of Animals, whales today are killed by explosive harpoons, which enter the whale near the head and explode inside its body. However, this method is far from effective, as shown by the fact that only about 40% of the whales harpooned die immediately (2). In addition, these hunting methods go against modern society's acceptable standard of animal suffering. Benson found that "people surveyed around the world now correctly understand that whales are intelligent, social mammals, not fish, and if hunted, must receive instant, painless death" (88). Commercial whalers have shown that they cannot meet this international ethical standard, and thus this practice must stop.

Information 1 is a fact about the common whaling method, and it is an example of the first supporting point, that the method of whaling is brutal. **Information 2** is a statistic that shows the ineffectiveness of whaling methods. **Information 3** is an expert's opinion which supports the second supporting point that most people worldwide find the killing methods unacceptable.

When choosing information to use in your essay, consider the following:
- Is the information relevant to your argument?
- Is the information specific enough?
- Does the information provide an example, statistical evidence or an expert's opinion that supports your argument?

Compare the following examples.

Supporting point 1:
The method of whaling is brutal and ineffective.

Information from outside sources:

✓ *Whales today are killed by explosive harpoons, which enter the whale near the head and explode inside its body.*

✗ *Walker says that the method of whaling used by major whaling countries is painful to whales.* (too general)

✗ *The International Whaling Commission (IWC) permits countries to conduct whaling for research purposes.* (irrelevant to the argument)

Supporting point 2:
Whales suffer unnecessary pain through the process of being hunted.

Information from outside sources:

✓ *"People surveyed around the world now correctly understand that whales are intelligent, social mammals, not fish, and if hunted, must receive instant, painless death" (88).*

✗ *Whales are known for their high intelligence.* (too general)

✗ *Female whales usually give birth once in two or three years. They nurse their calves for over a year, which helps develop a strong bond between mothers and infants.* (irrelevant to the argument)

Exercise 1

Look at body paragraphs 2 and 3 of the sample essay about whaling (page 95) and complete these tasks.

1. Underline all the information that comes from outside sources.

2. Identify the writer's idea which the information supports.

Exercise 2

The following two arguments are found in an essay about the topic "Can tigers and humans coexist?" Read each argument and the three pieces of information from outside sources. Choose the information that supports the argument most effectively. Explain your choice.

Argument 1:
It is true that tigers sometimes wander into villages and attack people.

Information from outside sources:
a. Tigers are shy by nature and rarely attack people.
b. In October 2006, a tiger wandered into a village in the Sundarbans wetlands in north east India, and killed three people.
c. Even deep in the Sundarbans mangroves river system, fishermen in small boats have been attacked because tigers are strong swimmers.

Argument 2:
The Indian government has introduced several programs to prevent contact between local villagers and tigers.

Information from outside sources:

a. In a recent national survey, 82% of Indians fully supported the government spending money on tiger preservation projects.

b. An official in the Ministry of Environment and Forests stated, "The tiger has been of highly symbolic and cultural value to Indians for thousands of years, and is considered a natural treasure."

c. The government subsidizes a project whereby villagers periodically release livestock into the forest for tigers to eat in order to discourage them from entering villages.

Section 3 — Presenting information from outside sources

When you include information from an outside source in your essay, present it using the correct format. There are three ways to present information from an outside source in your essay: **paraphrasing**, **summarizing** and **quoting**. By using these methods, you can avoid plagiarism (see page 81). The table below shows how the three methods are similar and different.

	Paraphrasing	Summarizing	Quoting
How do you paraphrase, summarize or quote?	• Rewrite the original text in your own words. • Change the sentence structure and vocabulary.	• Choose the most important parts of the original text and rewrite them in your own words. • Change the sentence structure and vocabulary.	• Present the original text as it is. • Do not make any changes to the sentence structure or vocabulary.
How do you present the writing?	• Do not use quotation marks.	• Do not use quotation marks.	• Put the original text between two quotation marks "…".
When do you use it?	• You want to use all the ideas of the original text. • The original is up to three sentences long.	• You want to use only the most important parts of the original text. • The original text is longer than three sentences.	• The original text is a powerful or elegant comment that leaves a strong impression on the reader.

Quoting

In addition to paraphrasing and summarizing, which you learned in Unit 3 Part 2, you can quote when you present information from outside sources. When you quote, present the original text in quotation marks (" "). The words in quotation marks must be exactly the same as the original; you must not change, add or omit any words.

Original text:

People surveyed around the world now correctly understand that whales are intelligent, social mammals, not fish, and if hunted, must receive instant, painless death.

Quotation:

*Benson found that "**people surveyed around the world now correctly understand that whales are intelligent, social mammals, not fish, and if hunted, must receive instant, painless death**" (88).*

When you use a reporting word with a quotation, use a comma instead of *that*. If the quotation is a complete sentence, begin with a capital letter:

*****Ellis states,** "For the Inupiat, whale hunting is more than just a means of sustaining life; it is their cultural heritage and a bond that unites them with their ancestors."*

Quoting is a very simple way to present information from outside sources. However, be careful not to overuse it. If your essay has too many quotations, it might give the reader the impression that you rely on them, or prefer other people's words more than your own. You should use a quotation only when the original writing is an impressive comment that supports your argument powerfully.

Exercise 3

The two statements below are found in an essay about "Tourism." Each statement needs to be supported by information from outside sources a–e. Choose one source that best supports each statement, and paraphrase, summarize, or quote each source. Use all or only part of the outside source, as appropriate. Introduce the paraphrase, summary, or quote after each statement using the author's name and a reporting verb. See Unit 3, Part 2 (page 85).

Statement 1:

Air pollution is a major problem in many national parks where motor vehicles are regular means of transportation for tourists.

_____

_____

_____

_____

_____

_____

Statement 2:

Tourism has posed serious threats to the rich marine life in coastal resorts around the world.

_____

_____

_____

_____

_____

_____

Information from outside sources to be paraphrased, summarized, or quoted:

a. For the 49 least developed countries in the world, found mainly in Africa and Asia, the tourism industry ranks second only to oil exports for their main source of revenue.

Author: Johnson

b. Of the 109 countries with coral reefs, 90 report increasing damage to reefs due to tourism; coral is being killed by individual divers breaking off chunks for souvenirs, organized commercial harvesting, and by cruise ships dropping anchors and sewage onto reefs.

Author: Taylor

c. Although natural wonders are commonly considered a nation's treasures, historic and culturally significant buildings are equally valuable assets of national heritage. Unfortunately, of the 20,000 structures protected under the National Heritage Mandate, more than 25% are in danger of being lost without immediate repair or restoration.

Author: Johnson

d. Because tourism is crucially important to Hawaii, the state has created new laws to protect and preserve both its rainforest and coral reefs, and all the native plant, animal, and marine species dependent on them. Due to this, Hawaii has become an important center for international research into ecological systems and sustainability.

Author: Taylor

e. Although vehicle emissions have been significantly reduced over the past decades, motor vehicles still account for almost half of the greenhouse gases in the United States. In addition, trucks and buses running on diesel fuel release fine sulfur particles into the air. In several parts of the country, especially California, these emissions are the greatest source of pollution in parks. Almost every major national park in California, from Yosemite in the north to Joshua Tree in the south, suffers from air pollution caused by vehicle emissions.

Author: Taylor

Review questions

1. What should you be careful of when you choose information from outside sources?

2. What are the three ways to present information from outside sources in your essay?

3. What are the differences between them?

4. When should you use quotations?

3 | Editing a research essay

The goals of this lesson:

- Making accurate generalizations
- Editing a research essay

Section 1   Making accurate generalizations

The purpose of a research essay is to persuade the reader to accept your position. For this purpose, you should support your arguments with strong evidence. At the same time, make sure that your arguments are stated accurately. For example, read the following statement from a research essay about the topic "Can tigers and humans coexist?"

People should be allowed to shoot tigers that wander into villages because these tigers attack farm animals and villagers.

In this statement, the writer is making a **generalization** about tigers. He says that they attack farm animals and villagers. However, this generalization is not accurate. It might be true that *some* tigers that wander into villages attack farm animals and people, but not *all* of them. In other words, this statement is an **overgeneralization**, where the writer makes a claim about all members of a group, but it is only true for some members. Overgeneralizations are, therefore, inaccurate and will weaken your argument because the reader can easily doubt what you are saying, and may even think that you do not understand your topic.

Thus, when you make a generalization, you should check if it is accurate. If you realize that you have overgeneralized, you should rewrite the statement. For example, the statement above can be rewritten as follows:

People should be allowed to shoot tigers that wander into villages because these tigers might *attack farm animals and villagers.*

The following structures can be used to make accurate generalizations.

1. Expressions of quantity

More likely ←——————————————————————————→ Less likely

a majority of most (of)*	many (of) a number of a lot of*	some (of)*	few (of) little**

These words and phrases are placed before nouns. They are usually used with countable nouns, but the expressions with asterisks (*) can be used with both countable and uncountable nouns. (**Little* is used with uncountable nouns only.)

✗ *People should be allowed to shoot tigers that wander into villages because these tigers attack farm animals and villagers.*

✓ *People should be allowed to shoot tigers that wander into villages because **some of** these tigers attack farm animals and villagers.*

✗ *Animals born in zoos develop behavioral problems.*

✓ ***Many** animals born in zoos develop behavioral problems.*

✗ *People do not know how farm animals are slaughtered.*

✓ ***Few** people know how farm animals are slaughtered.*

2. Adverbs of frequency

More likely ←——————————————————————————→ Less likely

usually generally	often frequently	sometimes occasionally	rarely seldom

As a general rule, adverbs of frequency go before the main verb. However, when the main verb is *be*, they go after it.

✗ *People should be allowed to shoot tigers that wander into villages because these tigers attack farm animals and villagers.*

✓ *People should be allowed to shoot tigers that wander into villages because these tigers **sometimes** attack farm animals and villagers.*

✗ *Japanese people today do not eat whale meat.*

✓ *Japanese people today **rarely** eat whale meat.*

✗ *Laboratory animals are killed when the research is over.*

✓ *Laboratory animals are **often** killed when the research is over.*

3. May, might, tend to, be likely to

More likely ←——————————————————————————————→ Less likely

	tend to be likely to	may might	

May and *might* are used to show that something is possible. They are modal auxiliaries and should be placed before the main verb.

✗ *People should be allowed to shoot tigers that wander into villages because these tigers attack farm animals and villagers.*

✓ *People should be allowed to shoot tigers that wander into villages because these tigers **may** attack farm animals and villagers.*

✗ *Breeding programs in zoos save endangered species such as the giant panda.*

✓ *Breeding programs in zoos **might** save endangered species such as the giant panda.*

In negative sentences, *may not* or *might not* is used.

Tend to and *be likely to* indicate that something is probable. They are followed by a verb.

✗ *Laboratory animals are killed when the research is over.*

✓ *Laboratory animals **tend to** be killed when the research is over.*

✗ *Animals born in zoos develop behavioral problems.*

✓ *Animals born in zoos **are likely to** develop behavioral problems.*

In negative sentences, *tend not to* or *not likely to* is used.

Exercise 1

Rewrite the following generalizations to make them more accurate.

1. Zoos are creating more natural environments for their animals.

2. People living in cities keep their dogs in small apartments and do not give them enough exercise.

3. Horses have to be destroyed after breaking their leg during a race.

4. Animals born in zoos cannot survive in the wild.

5. When buying clothes that use fur, people do not think how the animals were killed.

6. Dogs and cats abandoned by their owners end up in animal shelters.

Section 2   Editing a research essay

When you edit a research essay, it is important to check:
- if the position is stated clearly.
- if it is supported by strong evidence.

For information from outside sources, check whether:
- the information is paraphrased, summarized or quoted appropriately.
- the sources are identified using the correct citation format.

Research Essay Editing Checklist

- **First reading: check for content and organization**

Content
1. Is the writer's position clear and consistent throughout the essay?
2. Does the information from outside sources support the writer's arguments effectively?

Organization
Introductory paragraph
1. Do the building sentences give background on the topic?
2. Does the thesis statement state the writer's position and three main arguments?

Body paragraphs
3. Do the topic sentences of the body paragraphs state the writer's main arguments? Do they also include the writer's position?

Concluding paragraph
4. Does the concluding paragraph restate the thesis statement and summarize the body paragraphs?
5. Is the writer's final thought presented at the end? Is it relevant to the essay topic?

- **Second reading: check for citation grammar and style**

Citation
1. Is the information from outside sources paraphrased, summarized or quoted appropriately?
2. Is the information cited in the main text? Does the in-text citation follow the correct format?
3. Is there a Works Cited list on a separate page? Does it follow the correct format?
4. Do the sources in the list match those cited in the main text?

Grammar and style
1. Are conjunctions used correctly?
2. Are transitional expressions used effectively?
3. Are pronouns used correctly?
4. Are the overgeneralizations avoided?
5. Is the style of writing appropriate for an academic essay?

Edit the following first draft using the checklist on the previous page.

Step 1 Read the draft once to check the content and organization, and write some comments. Be sure to:
- comment on both the strengths and weaknesses of the draft.
- suggest a way to improve any weaknesses.

Step 2 Read the draft again to check citation, grammatical errors and style problems. Write your corrections on the draft.

Topic:
Should people be allowed to kill animals for their fur?

Killing Animals for Fur

Nowadays, wearing animal fur is back in fashion. Many people wear coat and jacket bordered with fur. Fur is also used for shoes, hats, gloves, and scarves. People buy these items because they are fashionable and warm. Although some people are against it, humans should be allowed to kill animals for their fur because it is a natural thing for them and fur is special material that cannot be replaced by artificial material.

First, humans should be allowed to kill animals for their fur because it is a natural thing for them. Humans have always used animal fur as clothing. For example, according to James Radcliffe, early humans wore fur tens of thousands of years ago (53). Even now, wearing fur is a part of daily life for some people. For instance, the Inuit people living in Arctic coastal areas wear boots and other clothing made from caribou or sealskin to protect themselves from cold weather ("The Inuit"). Compared to the long history of fur clothes, the idea that wearing fur is wrong or killing animals is cruel is recent idea. In short, humans should be allowed to kill animals and use their fur because it is their natural way of life.

Second, fur is very special material that cannot be replaced by artificial material. Natural fur looks and feels different from artificial fur. Kenny says, when she wears fur, people usually compliment it and want to touch it. In addition, natural fur is more ecological than artificial fur. Fake fur is made of synthetic fabrics such as acrylic and polyester, which are chemical substances. In order to produce them, we have to use a large amount of oil. Furthermore, it is not easy to dispose of them. Because if they are burned, they emit poisonous gas. In contrast, fur is easer to produce and is more durable. For example, women wear fur coat they inherited from their grandmothers or great grandmothers.

Moreover, similar to my last point is that fur is a natural, renewable resource so using it does not harm the environment. In Fur Over the Years it says that fur comes from animals which are raised on farms specifically for that purpose. It is no different than cows, pigs, chickens or salmon which are raised on farms only so we can eat them. Very few wild animals are used relative to the amount of fur produced. Even in cases where wild animals are used, like with seals, the number killed is closely controlled so the population of the seals is not negatively affected. In both cases, there is no bad effect on the environment or animal populations. And, the supply of fur is safely produced year after year.

In conclusion, people should be allowed to kill animals for their fur. It is natural way of life that has continued for thousands of years. Moreover, real fur is better quality and more ecological than artificial fur. It is sad to think about killing cute animals, but we cannot help it because that is our way of life.

Works Cited

Radcliffe, James. *Fur Over the Years*. Vancouver: Northern Pacific University Press 2006.

Thompson, Joshua. "The Inuit: Traditions and Realities." *Modern Anthropology* Sept. 2004: 24–31.

Kenny, Mary. "Why I'm a Foxy Lady." The Guardian Newspaper Online. 19 Jan. 2006. Accessed 2 Feb. 2007 <http://www.guardian.co.uk/animalrights/story/ 0,,1689814,00.html>.

Review questions

1. What words and phrases can you use to make accurate generalizations?

2. What should you check when you edit a research essay?

Appendix A

Capitalization rules

1. **Capitalize proper nouns.**

   a. Names of people:
   Jane Austen   Dae-jung Kim   Simon Bolivar   Martin Luther King, Jr.

   b. Names of organizations and other groups of people:
   the United Nations   the Ministry of Economy, Trade and Industry
   Cambridge University   Amnesty International   Apple Computer
   the Beatles   the New York Yankees

   c. Names of places:
   London   Mexico City   Beijing   New Zealand   the United States
   the Pacific Ocean   Lake Baikal   Mt. Everest   the Nile
   North America   the Middle East   Asia

   d. Nationalities, ethnic groups, languages, and religions:
   Thai   Russian   African American   Arabic   Muslim   Buddhism

   e. Days and months:
   Monday   November   St. Valentine's Day   Christmas   New Year's Day

2. **Capitalize the first word, the last word and all the important words in titles. Do not capitalize the following words unless they are the first or last word:**
   - articles (*a*, *an*, *the*)
   - coordinate conjunctions (e.g., *and*, *but*, *or*)
   - prepositions (e.g., *of*, *in*, *on*, *with*)
   - *to* in infinitives (e.g., **to** *go*, **to** *play*)

   a. The title of your own essay:
   Reasons for Going to University   The Social Habits of Killer Whales and Dolphins

   b. The title of someone else's work cited in your essay:
   - Use an <u>underline</u> or *italics* for the title of a book, magazine, newspaper, website, movie, play or TV program:
     <u>The Lord of the Rings</u> or *The Lord of the Rings*
     <u>New York Times</u> or *New York Times*
     (When citing a newspaper or magazine, omit any article (*a*, *an*, *the*) at the beginning of the title.)
   - Use quotation marks for the title of an article in a newspaper, magazine or website:
     "Evolution of Whales"   "The Himalayas: Journey to the End of the World"

3. **Do not capitalize entire words unless they are acronyms:**
   ✓ UNHCR   UNICEF   IBM
   ✗ CAMBRIDGE UNIVERSITY   THE BEATLES   <u>TIME</u>   *STAR WARS*

Appendix B

Conjunctions

Conjunctions are used to **connect two sentences** into one and show how the two clauses relate to one another.

Coordinating conjunctions

| independent clause | + comma + **coordinating conjunction** + | independent clause |

Working part-time gives students extra spending money, **and** *it helps them learn about society.*

Subordinating conjunctions

| **subordinating conjunction** + subject + verb | + comma + | independent clause |

dependent clause

Because *parking space is limited in universities, very few students go to school by car.*

| independent clause | + | **subordinating conjunction** + subject + verb |

dependent clause

Very few university students in large cities go to school by car *because parking space on campuses is limited.*

Function	Coordinating conjunctions	Subordinating conjunctions
Showing a similar idea	*and*	*as*
Showing an opposite or contrasting idea	*but*	*although* *even though* *whereas* *while*
Showing a cause or reason		*as* *because* *since*
Showing a purpose		*so that*
Showing an effect or result	*so*	
Showing a condition		*if* *unless**
Showing an alternative	*or*	
Showing a time relationship		*after* *as* *as soon as* *before* *since* *until* *when* *while*

* *Unless* expresses the idea of "if not."

Appendix C

Transitional expressions

Transitional expressions show **how one sentence is related to the previous sentence.**

1. **Adverbs or adverbial phrases** are used at the beginning of a sentence, followed by a comma:
    People with university degrees find good jobs. <u>Therefore</u>, many parents send their children to universities.

2. **Prepositional phrases (preposition + noun)** are used at the beginning of a sentence, followed by a comma:
    <u>Unlike</u> <u>high schools</u>, universities allow students to choose a major.

3. **Noun phrases (adjective + noun)** are usually used as a subject:
    <u>Another</u> <u>reason</u> for going to university is that a college education leads to a better future career.

Function	Transitional expressions		
	Adverbs or adverbial phrases	**Prepositional phrases** (preposition + noun)	**Noun phrases** (adjective + noun)
Listing ideas	*first* *second* *third* *finally*		*one ...* *another ...* *the first ...* *the second ...* *the third ...* *the last ...*
Adding an idea	*also* *furthermore* *in addition* *moreover*	*besides ...* *in addition to ...*	*another ...*
Showing a similar idea	*also* *likewise* *similarly*	*like ...*	
Showing an opposite idea or contrasting idea	*however* *in comparison* *in contrast* *nevertheless* *on the other hand*	*compared to/with ...* *despite ...* *in spite of ...* *unlike ...*	
Showing an effect or result	*accordingly* *as a result* *consequently* *therefore* *thus*	*because of ...* *due to ...*	
Showing an example	*for example* *for instance*		
Emphasizing an idea	*in fact* *indeed*		
Restating the idea in the previous sentence	*in other words*		
Concluding or summarizing	*in brief* *in conclusion* *in short* *in summary* *to sum up* *to summarize*		

Appendix D

Using information from outside sources (summary)

Read related articles and choose the information that you will use in your essay.

Decide how you will present the information in your essay:

a. The original writing is short (up to three sentences) and you want to use all the ideas – **paraphrase the information.** (See pages 73–76.)

b. The original text is long (more than three sentences) and you want to use only the most important ideas – **summarize the information** (See pages 76–80.)

c. The original writing uses powerful or elegant expression. You want to use it as it is – **quote the information.** (See page 109–111.)

Cite the source of the information in the essay (in-text citation):

- You have the author's name and the page number. = A
- You have the author's name but not the page number. = B
- You do not have the author's name. = C

A

Give the author's name using a reporting word. Give the page number in parentheses at the end of the sentence.

OR

Give the author's name and the page number in parentheses at the end of the sentence. (See page 83.)

B

Give the author's name using a reporting word. (See page 83.)

C

Give the title of the article in parentheses at the end of the sentence. If you have the page number, put it after the title in the parentheses. (See page 84.)

Write a Works Cited list entry for the source.

Find the correct MLA format for the type of source on page 87–89.

Language Choice

Contents

GET READY MODULE: LANGUAGE CHOICE 1-6

PRACTICE

1 Personal information **Complete the dialogue.**

A: Hello, I'm Sarah. What's your name?
B: My ¹ _name_ is Jorge Gómez.
A: Where are you from?
B: I'm ²_____ Brazil.
A: How old are you?
B: I'm fifteen ³_____ old.
A: And what's your address?
B: My ⁴_____ is 37 Pessoa Street,
   Sao Paolo, Brazil.
A: What's your telephone number?
B: My phone ⁵_____ is 55 03 22 717
   623.

2 *to be* **Complete the dialogue.**

A: Hello, my name ¹ _is_ Kristin. ²_____
   you Chris?
B: No, I'm ³_____ . My name's Ben.
   Chris ⁴_____ the school secretary
   and I ⁵_____ a teacher.
A: ⁶_____ I in your class?
B: Yes, you ⁷_____ . Come and meet
   three students: Adam, Novak and Diana.
   They are really nice.
A: ⁸_____ they in my class?
B: Adam ⁹_____ but Novak and Diana
   ¹⁰_____ in a different class.

3 *Wh-* questions **Write questions for these answers.**

1 A: _Where are you from_?
  B: I'm from Australia.
2 A: _____ ?
  B: It's 0584 8798 9999.
3 A: _____ ?
  B: My name's Joanna Birch.
4 A: _____ ?
  B: I'm fourteen years old.
5 A: _____ ?
  B: My teacher is Sarah.
6 A: _____ ?
  B: 31 Park Street, Orleton.

4 Subject pronouns and possessive adjectives **Use the cues and the words in brackets to write sentences.**

1 name / Tim / from London (his/he)
  His name's Tim. He's from London .
2 sixteen years old / name / Alice (she/her)
  _____ .
3 language students / teacher / Frances (they/their)
  _____ .
4 names / Juana and Monica / from Spain (our/we)
  _____ .
5 telephone number / 0927 6545 6777 / from Oxford (my/I)
  _____ .
6 name? / from Britain? (your/you)
  _____ ?

5 Imperatives **Complete the exam instructions with the words below.**

write   listen to   don't (x 2)   ~~use~~
read   match   answer

1 Don't _use_ a dictionary in the exam.
2 _____ the text and _____ the questions.
3 _____ the dialogue and _____ the photos with the sentences.
4 _____ speak in the exam and _____ tell your partner the answers.
5 _____ your name on the exam paper.

6 *can/can't* **Complete the sentences about the drawings.**

1 Anna _can play the piano_ and she _____ .

4 John _____ .
  He _____ .

2 Carl _____ and he _____ .

5 Katy _____ .
  She _____ .

3 Pete _____ .
  He _____ .

REFERENCE

Personal information

My name's Jamie Smith. *I'm from* Britain.
I'm fifteen **years old**. *My address is* 19 Mill Street,
Bristol. *My phone number is* 0207 733 1587 (oh, two,
oh, seven, seven, three, three, one, five, eight, seven.)

to be

We can use the verb *to be* **to give personal information:**

Affirmative
I **am** *from Argentina.*
You/We/They **are** *sixteen years old.*
He/She/It **is** *from Canada.*

Negative
I **am not** *from Bulgaria.*
You/We/They **are not** *twenty years old.*
He/She/It **is not** *from Italy.*

Yes/No Questions
Am *I a student?*
Are you *from Spain?*
Is *she a teacher?*

Short answers	
Yes, I **am**.	*No, I'm* **not**.
Yes, you **are**.	*No, you* **aren't**.
Yes, she **is**.	*No, she* **isn`t**.

Wh- questions

Asking about things: **What**'s your name / telephone number / address?
Asking about places: **Where** are you from?
Asking about age: **How old** are you?
Asking about people: **Who** is my teacher?

Subject pronouns and possessive adjectives

Subject pronouns	Possessive adjectives
I'm a student.	**My** name's Jamie.
You are in my class.	What's **your** name?
He's a teacher.	**His** name is Colin.
She's from London.	**Her** telephone number is 0207 8665 8864.
It is 13 Mill Street.	**Its** name is Bath School.
We're from Britain.	**Our** teacher is Sarah.
You are in my class.	**Your** teacher is Tom.
They are in your class.	**Their** names are Anna and Karol.

Imperatives

We use the infinitive without *to* **for positive commands:**
Read the text. **Listen to** the dialogue. **Ask** and **answer** questions.

We use *don't* **+ infinitive without** *to* **for negative commands:**
Don't look at the answers.
Don't speak in Polish.

can/can't

We use *can* **to talk about abilities:**
I **can** play the guitar and sing.
I **can't** ride a horse or swim 100 metres.

Affirmative
I / You / He / She / It / We / You / They **can** *swim and ski.*

Negative
I / You / He / She / It / We / You / They **can't** (**cannot**) *play an instrument.*

Questions
Can *I / you / he / she / it / we / you / they play football?*

Short answers
Yes, I/he/she/we/they **can**.
No, I/he/she/we/they **can't**. (**cannot**)

PRACTICE

❼ *this, that, these, those* **Look at the drawings and complete the sentences.**

1 _This_ is my new mobile phone.
2 _Those_ shoes are very old.
3 _____ books are for my English class.
4 _____ computer is new but it is very expensive.
5 _____ new MP3 player is great.
6 _____ are my new earrings.

❽ **Possessive** *'s* **Add the apostrophe to the sentences below.**

1 Those photos are my mums.
   Those photos are my mum's.
2 That violin is Francess - she's my sister.
3 Those toys are our dogs - their names are Homer and Maggie.
4 My dads name is Colin.
5 My parents books are very interesting.
6 Those computers are my brothers - their names are Alan and Roy.

❾ **Possessive pronouns Choose the correct word to complete the sentences.**

1 (My)/mine name is Fred and that book is *my/mine*.
2 That dictionary is not *your/yours* - it is *my/mine*!
3 My sister is sixteen and *her/hers* name is Silvia. Those earrings are *her/hers*.
4 We are in Class 10A and *our/ours* teacher is Mrs Marsh. That classroom is *our/ours*.
5 Joe and Sam are *my/mine* friends. Those MP3 players are *their/theirs*.
6 Who is *your/yours* teacher? Is that classroom *your/yours*?

❿ *have/has got* **Use the cues to write sentences.**

1 Monica / got / blue eyes and blond hair
   Monica has got blue eyes and blond hair.
2 I / not got / blue eyes
3 you / got / brothers or sisters?
4 We / got / a new teacher
5 Ken and Stuart / not got / long hair
6 your sister / got / dark hair?

⓫ **Times Write down the times.**

1 7.05 _five past seven_   2 1.45 _____

3 9.00 _____   4 3.35 _____

5 11.30 _____   6 6.20 _____

⓬ **Object pronouns Choose the correct pronouns to complete the sentences.**

1 (She)/Her is my sister. Talk to *she/her*.
2 Tell *us/we* the answer. *We/us* don't understand.
3 *I/me* can use computers. Ask *I/me* a question about *they/them*.
4 Alan is in my class and *he/him* is my friend. Look at this photo of *he/him*.
5 *They/them* are our teachers. Listen to *they/them*.

REFERENCE

this, that, these, those

We use *this* (singular) and *these* (plural) for people and things near us:
This jacket is expensive. *These* photos are great.

We use *that* (singular) and *those* (plural) for people and things that are not so near to us:
That painting is beautiful. *Those* shoes are cheap.

Possessive 's

We use *'s* at the end of a noun to say that something belongs to a person, is related to them or is part of them:
That is Elizabeth's computer. (it is her computer)

We add *'s* to singular nouns:
This is Tom's mobile phone.

We add *'* to plural nouns that end in *s*:
My grandparents' house is in London.

Possessive pronouns

Possessive adjectives	Possessive pronouns
This is **my** piano.	This piano is **mine**.
That is **your** hat.	That hat is **yours**.
That is **his** guitar.	That guitar is **his**.
Those are **her** shoes.	Those shoes are **hers**.
These are **our** books.	These books are **ours**.
That is **their** car.	That car is **theirs**.

have/has got

We use *have/has got* to talk about possessions:
I've got a new computer.
We use *have/has got* for descriptions of appearance:
He's got blue eyes and dark hair.

Affirmative
I/You/We/They**'ve got** (**have got**) long hair.
He/She/It**'s got** (**has got**) a nice smile.
Negative
I/You/We/They **haven't got** (**have not got**) a sister.
He/She/It **hasn't got** (**has not got**) green eyes.
Questions
Have I/you/we/they **got** brothers or sisters?
Has he/she/it **got** dark hair?
Short answers
Yes, I/you/we/they **have**. No, I/you/we/they **haven't**.
Yes, he/she/it **has**. No, he/she/it **hasn't**.

Times

10.00 - ten o'clock

11.05 - five past eleven

12.15 - quarter past twelve

1.30 - half past one

1.35 - twenty-five to two

3.45 - quarter to four

4.50 - ten to five

6.00 - six o'clock

Object pronouns

Subject pronouns	Object pronouns
I've got long hair.	Look at **me**.
You can speak French.	Can I ask **you** a question?
He is our teacher.	Tell **him** the answer.
She is my sister.	Listen to **her**.
It is a letter in English.	Answer questions about **it**.
You are new students.	Can I speak to **you**?
We don't understand that.	Can you tell **us** the answer?
They are your partners.	Tell **them** about your interests.

PRACTICE

13 Interests and free time **Complete the sentences with the verbs below.**

| use | go | play | watch | ~~chat~~ | go to |

1 In the evening, I _chat_ with my friends online.
2 On Saturday, I _____ shopping.
3 In the evening, I _____ the cinema.
4 On Sunday, I _____ tennis with my dad.
5 In the afternoon, I _____ the internet.
6 In the evening, I _____ TV.

14 Present Simple **Use the cues to make sentences in the Present Simple.**

1 My friends / not speak Spanish
   My friends don't speak Spanish.

2 We / go out at weekends
   _____

3 Young people / love sport
   _____

4 My mother / work in a bank
   _____

5 My sister / not do housework
   _____

6 I / not live in a big city
   _____

7 My dog / not like cats
   _____

8 You / not know me
   _____

15 Adverbs of frequency **Use the cues to make sentences in the Present Simple. Put the adverbs in the correct place.**

1 I / be happy / always
   I am always happy.

2 My friend / study / never
   _____

3 My brothers / watch football on TV / often
   _____

4 We / go to parties / sometimes
   _____

5 My parents / be at home on Saturday / usually
   _____

6 He / be tired in the evening / never
   _____

7 I / speak English / often
   _____

8 My teacher / use the computer / sometimes
   _____

16 *like* for examples **Use the words in brackets to rewrite the sentences.**

1 They hunt animals. (kangaroos and lizards)
   They hunt animals, like kangaroos and lizards.

2 I play sports. (basketball and golf)
3 In my bag I've got things. (my mobile phone and my MP3 player)
4 We study interesting subjects. (English and history)
5 Australia has got interesting cities. (Sydney and Melbourne)
6 They are from different countries. (Spain and Italy)

17 Plurals **Complete the sentences with plurals.**

1 My teacher has got two _children_ . (child)
2 On Wednesday, we have got six _____ . (class)
3 On Saturday, I often go to _____ . (party)
4 At home, we've got a lot of _____ . (book)
5 That toilet is for _____ . (woman)
6 I often chat with _____ online. (person)

18 Present Simple: questions **Write questions to ask about the <u>underlined</u> words.**

1 I read newspapers <u>every day</u>.
   How often do you read newspapers?

2 My father buys <u>books</u> online.
   _____

3 We spend weekends <u>at home</u>.
   _____

4 My teachers start work at <u>8 a.m.</u>.
   _____

5 I like <u>computer games</u>.
   _____

6 My cousin meets <u>his friends</u> in a café.
   _____

7 My sisters <u>never</u> play tennis.
   _____

8 My dog loves <u>toys</u>.
   _____

REFERENCE

Interests and free time

*I **like computer games** and **photography**.*
*In the morning, I **listen to music** and **use the internet**.*
*In the afternoon, I **play football** and **go running**.*
*In the evening, I **watch TV** and **listen to music**.*
*On Saturday, I **go shopping** and **go swimming**.*
*In the afternoon, I **go to the cinema**.*

Present Simple

We use the Present Simple to talk about:

- **things that happen regularly**
*I **start** school at 8 a.m.*
*She **plays** tennis on Saturdays.*
*My friends **don't go out** very often.*

- **things that are true in general:**
*My grandparents **live** in Sweden.*
*I **don't like** sport.*
*My sister **knows** a lot of interesting people.*

Affirmative
*I/You/We/They **like** sport.*
*He/She/It **likes** sport.*
Negative
*I/You/We/They **don't like** sport.*
*He/She/It **doesn't like** sport.*
Questions
***Do** I/you/we/they **like** sport?*
***Does** he/she/it **like** sport?*
***How often do** you **go out**?*
***When does** your teacher **use** the internet?*
Short Answers
*Yes, I/you/we/they **do**.*
*No, I/you/we/they **don't**.*
*Yes, he/she/it **does**.*
*No, he/she/it **doesn't**.*

Adverbs of frequency

We use these adverbs of frequency with the Present Simple:

100%   0%

always   usually   often   sometimes   never

We put the adverbs of frequency after the verb *be* and before other verbs:
*He **is** usually nice.*
*He usually **goes** to bed early.*

Like for examples

*I often play sports, **like** football and tennis.*
*They buy things, **like** clothes and DVDs.*
*He's got interests, **like** photography and computers.*

Plurals

	Singular	Plural
+ s	house	houses
	village	villages
	bird	birds
	kangaroo	kangaroos
	computer game	computer games
	film	films
+ es	bus	buses
	church	churches
	class	classes
+ ies	party	parties
	story	stories
	family	families
	activity	activities
	dictionary	dictionaries
irregular	life	lives
	wife	wives
	man	men
	woman	women
	child	children
	person	people

PRACTICE

⑲ Describing homes Complete the description of a home.

Our flat ¹ _has_ got four bedrooms. My ²_____ room is the kitchen. ³_____ has got white walls and a grey floor. It's got a cooker, a microwave, a dishwasher and a washing ⁴_____ . It's a great ⁵_____ to relax. I like my home ⁶_____ it's tidy and comfortable.

⑳ there is/are Complete the dialogue with *there is* or *there are.*

A: Is your room big, Jane?
B: It's small but ¹ _there is_ a big window.
A: ²_____ any furniture?
B: Oh yes, ³_____ a bed, a desk and ⁴_____ bookshelves.
A: ⁵_____ a wardrobe?
B: Yes, ⁶_____ . And ⁷_____ nice curtains.
A: What ⁸_____ on the walls?
B: ⁹_____ photos of my family and friends. And ¹⁰_____ a *Star Trek* poster.

㉑ some/any Complete the sentences with *some* or *any*.

1 There aren't _any_ plants in my bedroom but I've got _____nice pictures.
2 Have you got _____ CDs?
3 We've got _____ good friends in Scotland.
4 There aren't _____ bookshelves in the living room. Maybe they've got _____ books in their bedrooms.
5 Are there _____ comfortable armchairs here?
6 We haven't got _____ curtains in the living room.

㉒ Multi-part verbs (1) Complete the description.

I usually wake ¹ _up_ at seven o'clock and get ²_____ at quarter past seven. I have breakfast and listen to the radio. Then I go ³_____ at eight o'clock. I get ⁴_____ home at three o'clock. In the afternoon, I look ⁵_____ our dog, Jimmy. I do my homework and chat with my friends online. Then I go ⁶_____ bed at 11.00. I go ⁷_____ sleep at five past eleven - I am usually very tired!

㉓ Prepositions of place *in/on/at* Choose the correct preposition to complete the sentence.

1 The washing machine is *in/on* the bathroom.
2 The lamp is *in/on* the table.
3 My mum is *in/at* the living room.
4 My dad is *in/at* work.
5 The fruit is *in/on* the fridge.
6 The posters are *in/on* the wall.
7 My sister is *in/at* Italy.
8 My brother is *in/at* the bathroom.

㉔ a lot of/no/how much/how many Complete the sentences with *a lot of, no, much, many* or *a/an.*

1 In my room there are _no_ posters of pop stars but I love football and I've got _____ photos of Lionel Messi.
2 How _____ money have you got? Can we buy _____ CD?
3 My room is small, there's _____ room for a big desk but I've got _____ armchair.
4 Our home isn't modern - there are _____ computers but we've got _____ books.
5 How _____ bathrooms are there in your home? There are _____ people in my family so we've got three bathrooms.

REFERENCE

Describing homes

Our flat has got three bedrooms.
My favourite room is the living room.
It has got green walls and white doors.
It's got two sofas, a TV and bookshelves.
It's a great place to relax.
I like my home because it's comfortable and light.

there is/are

We use *there is/there are* to say that something is or is not in a particular place.

Affirmative
There is a stereo system in my room.
There are nice restaurants in our town.

Negative
There isn't a swimming pool in my house.
There aren't any books in his room.

Questions	Short answers
Is there a TV in your room?	Yes, *there is.*/No, *there aren't*.
Are there bookshelves in your flat?	Yes, *there are.*/No, *there aren't*.

What carpet *is there* in your room?

Countable/Uncountable nouns

English nouns can be countable or uncountable.

Countable nouns:
- can be singular or plural
  man - men, chair - chairs, house - houses
- can go with numbers
  I've got one friend.
  There are eleven players in a football team.

Uncountable nouns:
- are always singular and go with singular verbs
  Money is important.
  Water is expensive.
- don't take *a/an* in front of them
  I like milk and cheese.
- don't go with numbers
  I've got some time, I need money.

some/any

We use *some* and *any* in front of plural and uncountable nouns.
We usually use *any* in questions and negative sentences.
We usually use *some* in affirmative sentences.
*There is **some** juice in the fridge.*
*We haven't got **any** pets.*
*Are there **any** people outside?*
*Have you got **any** money?*

Multi-part verbs (1)

*I **wake up** at eight o'clock.*
*I **get up** at ten past eight.*
*I **go out** at half past eight.*
*My mum **looks after** my baby sister.*
*I **get back** home at four o'clock.*
*I **go to bed** at half past ten.*
*I **go to sleep** at a quarter to eleven.*

Prepositions of place: in/on/at

in
in a room:
*I am **in** the living room. My dad is **in** the kitchen.*
in a container:
*The apples are **in** the fridge. The dinner is **in** the oven.*
in a country:
*London is **in** the UK. New York is **in** the United States.*
on
on a surface:
*My bag is **on** the floor. The posters are **on** the wall.*
at
at a place:
*My sister is **at** the cinema. I am **at** home.*

a lot of/no

We use *a lot of* and *no* with plural nouns and uncountable nouns:
*I've got **a lot of** time.*
*There are **a lot of** plants in your room.*
*There's **no** cola in the fridge.*
*I've got **no** books about pirates.*

how much?/how many?

We use *how many* to ask about plural nouns:
How many chairs are there in the classroom?
We use *how much* to ask about uncountable nouns:
How much furniture is there in your living room?

MODULE 3: LANGUAGE CHOICE 25-30

PRACTICE

25 Going out **Complete the description.**

There are a lot of good night clubs and cafés
¹ _in_ my city. There aren't a ² _____ of good
sports centres or swimming pools. I ³ _____
going to outdoor markets and shopping centres.
My ⁴ _____ place is a small clothes shop. I like it
⁵ _____ it is cheap and the people are friendly. I
don't ⁶ _____ our local cinema because it's dark
and expensive.

26 Comparatives **Complete the sentences about the
two restaurants (Saigon and Venice) below with
the correct form of the adjective in brackets.**

Saigon

Venice

1 Venice is ___bigger___ than Saigon. (big)
2 Saigon is _____ than Venice. (expensive)
3 Saigon is _____ than Venice. (busy)
4 Venice is _____ than Saigon. (relaxed)
5 Saigon is _____ than Venice. (popular)
6 Venice is _____ than Saigon. (elegant)
7 Saigon is _____ than Venice.
   (comfortable)
8 Venice is _____ than Saigon. (quiet)

27 Comparatives **Complete the sentences with the
comparative form of the adjectives in brackets
and *than* to express your opinions.**

1 Big cities are _more interesting than_ small
   towns. (interesting)
2 Shopping centres are _____ small shops.
   (friendly)
3 Football is _____ basketball. (exciting)
4 A house is _____ a flat. (comfortable)
5 Rock music is _____ jazz. (modern)
6 Night clubs are _____ cafes. (expensive)

28 Verbs and prepositions **Complete the sentences.**

1 I listen _to_ music in the morning when I get up.
2 We always walk _____ the cinema.
3 In our art classes, we look _____ famous
   paintings.
4 On Sunday, I stay _____ home and relax.
5 Sometimes, my grandparents come _____
   our house and have lunch.
6 I live _____ a flat with three bedrooms.

29 Time prepositions **Complete the sentences.**

1 I play football _____ the weekend.
2 I study English _____ Tuesdays and
   Thursdays.
3 We go to Spain _____ the summer.
4 _____ Saturday morning, I go shopping.
5 I go to bed _____ eleven o'clock.
6 _____ the afternoon, I watch TV.

30 Superlatives **Complete the sentences with the
superlative form of the adjectives in brackets.**

1 London is _the most expensive_ city in the UK.
   (expensive)
2 Hyde Park is _____ park in London. (big)
3 The City has _____ buildings in London.
   (high)
4 Heathrow Airport is _____ in Europe.
   (busy)
5 Harrods is _____ shop in London. (famous)
6 The London Eye is _____ tourist attraction
   in London. (new)

REFERENCE

Going out

In my city, there are a lot of good shops and restaurants.
There aren't a lot of good theatres or museums.
I love going to cafés and night clubs.
My favourite place is a sports centre.
I like it because it is big and modern.
I don't like our local swimming pool *because it's* very busy.

Comparatives and superlatives

To compare people or things, we use the comparative form of the adjective and *than*:
*Paris is **smaller than** London but it's **more beautiful**.*
*My brother is **younger** and **less experienced than** me.*

To say that one person or thing is unique in a group, we use *the* and the superlative form of the adjective:
*New York is **the most exciting** town in the world.*
*I am **the oldest** student in my class.*

	Adjective	Comparative	Superlative
one syllable	nice old young small dark cheap	**nicer** **older** **younger** **smaller** **darker** **cheaper**	**the nicest** **the oldest** **the youngest** **the smallest** **the darkest** **the cheapest**
one syllable with a short vowel and a consonant	big fat hot thin	**bigger** **fatter** **hotter** **thinner**	**the biggest** **the fattest** **the hottest** **the thinnest**
-y at the end	busy pretty noisy friendly	**busier** **prettier** **noisier** **friendlier**	**the busiest** **the prettiest** **the noisiest** **the friendliest**
two or more syllables	famous expensive comfortable	**more/less famous** **more/less expensive** **more/less comfortable**	**the most/least famous** **the most/least expensive** **the most/least comfortable**
irregular	good bad	**better** **worse**	**the best** **the worst**

Verbs and prepositions

*I **live in** a small city in Britain.*
*I **stay at** home on Wednesday night and do my homework.*
*Then I often **listen to** music or watch TV.*
*I **go to** school at half-past eight. I usually **walk to** school.*
*On Saturday, my friends **come to** my house and we play computer games.*
*On Saturday afternoon, we **go around** the city centre and **look at** the clothes in the shops.*

Time prepositions

in
*I play tennis **in the morning**. **In the afternoon**, I relax at home. **In the evening**, I go out with my friends.*
***In the spring**, I play football. **In the summer**, I play tennis. I play basketball **in the autumn**. **In the winter**, I play computer games!*

on
***On Wednesdays**, I have my piano class. **On Friday**, I go to the cinema. **On Sunday**, I stay at home.*
***On Thursday mornings**, we have maths and science. I visit my grandmother **on Saturday afternoons**. **On Saturday night**, I go out with my friends.*

at
*I get up **at seven o'clock**. I have breakfast **at half-past seven**. I go out **at ten past eight**. **At the weekend**, I go to clubs and parties.*
*I never study **at night**. I relax and watch the TV.*

MODULE 4: LANGUAGE CHOICE 31–36

PRACTICE

31 **Birthday memories Complete the description.**

My birthday is ¹ _on_ the fifteenth
² _____ September. My earliest
birthday memory is my fifth birthday
³ _____ 1998. My best birthday ever
was ⁴ _____ September. There was a
party in a club ⁵ _____ my friends and
family. The dancing was ⁶ _____ !

32 **Past Simple: regular and irregular verbs Write the past form of the verbs below. Put *R* next to regular verbs and *I* next to irregular verbs.**

regular/ irregular	verb	Past Simple
_R_	arrive	_arrived_
____	ask	_____
____	be	_____
____	close	_____
____	come	_____
____	do	_____
____	find	_____
____	get	_____
____	give	_____
____	go	_____
____	have	_____
____	laugh	_____
____	like	_____
____	make	_____
____	play	_____
____	read	_____
____	say	_____
____	see	_____
____	speak	_____
____	take	_____
____	tell	_____
____	think	_____
____	work	_____
____	write	_____

33 **Past Simple Complete the text with the verbs in the Past Simple.**

My primary school ¹ _was_ (be) great and we ² _____ (love) it.
The lessons ³ _____ (be) always interesting and the teachers
⁴ _____ (not give) us a lot of homework. When we ⁵ _____
(have) a break, we ⁶ _____ (not stay) in the classroom but we
⁷ _____ (go) to the gym or ⁸ _____ (play) football outside.
We ⁹ _____ (do) a lot of projects and we often ¹⁰ _____
(visit) museums and ¹¹ _____ (meet) interesting people.
I ¹² _____ (not be) very good at science but I ¹³ _____
(not feel) bad about it because my teachers ¹⁴ _____ (be)
always very nice.

34 **Adverbs Choose the adjective or adverb to complete the sentences.**

1 My dad is a (good)/well tennis player. He always plays
   good/well.
2 I eat *quick/quickly*. I am a *quick/quickly* eater.
3 My sister talked to me *angry/angrily* because I used her
   computer. My sister was *angry/angrily* because I used her
   computer.
4 He is a very *slow/slowly* worker. He works very *slow/slowly*.
5 I am a *bad/badly* French student. I speak French *bad/badly*.
6 I was *nervous/nervously* when I walked to the exam. I walked
   nervous/nervously to the exam.

35 **Time linkers Choose the correct time linker to complete the sentences.**

1 (When)/After I came into the classroom, the teacher was at her
   desk.
2 I sat down *and then/when* started to read a book.
3 *After/Before* lunch, I was very hungry.
4 I got home at four o'clock. *When/Then* I started to do my
   homework.
5 I saw my old girlfriend *when/then* I went to the sports centre.
   She had her tennis racquet in her bag.
6 *After/Before* they arrived we talked to them.

36 **Past Simple: questions Read the sentences and write questions to ask about the missing information.**

1 I met ... at the bus stop.   Who _did you meet_ ?
2 They finished school at ... .   What time _____ ?
3 She bought ... .   What _____ ?
4 They bought ... hamburgers.   How many _____ ?
5 My mother found my mobile ... .   Where _____ ?
6 The accident happened ... .   When _____ ?
7 My parents went ... in 2010.   Where _____ ?
8 I was ... in 2010.   How old _____ ?

REFERENCE

Birthday memories

My birthday is on the fifth of April.
My earliest birthday memory is my fifth birthday in 1998.
My best birthday ever was last year.
There was a party at home with my friends and family.
The food *was great!*

Months

January, February, March, April, May, June, July, August, September, October, November, December

Ordinal numbers

First, second, third, fourth, fifth, sixth, seventh, eighth, ninth, tenth, eleventh, twelfth, thirteenth, fourteenth, fifteenth, sixteenth, seventeenth, eighteenth, nineteenth, twentieth, twenty-first, etc., thirtieth, fortieth, fiftieth, sixtieth, seventieth, eightieth, ninetieth, hundredth

Dates

10 January 1999 – 'the tenth of January, nineteen ninety-nine'
5 May 2008 – 'the fifth of May, two thousand and eight'
28 October 2012 – 'the twenty-eighth of October, twenty twelve'

Past Simple

We use the Past Simple to talk about events and finished situations from the past:
My primary school teachers *were* very good.
I *went* to school in Chicago.
He *smiled* and left the classroom.
We *didn't see* the accident.

Affirmative
I/You/He/She/It **liked** school.
We/They **found** some money.

Negative
I/You/He/She/It **didn't learn** Spanish.
We/They didn't **go** to dancing school.

Questions
Did I/you/he/she/it **like** PE classes?
Did we/they **like** PE classes

Short answers
Yes, I/you/he/she/it/we/they **did**.
No, I/you/he/she/it/we/they **didn't**.

English verbs can be regular (*stop, smile, play*) or irregular (*see, say, go*). (→ Irregular Verbs list, page 95)

Adverbs

We use adverbs of manner to describe an action or activity:
He worked **hard** and did **well** in his exam.
He **quickly** saw that it was Maggie.
They lived **happily** together for fifty-eight years.
Nervously, he walked over to her.

We also use adverbs to give our opinions about an action:
Sadly, Granddad died in 2009.

Regular	
	+ ly
bad	bad**ly**
slow	slow**ly**
quick	quick**ly**
nervous	nervous**ly**
sad	sad**ly**
	+ ily
angry	angr**ily**
noisy	nois**ily**
happy	happ**ily**
Irregular	
fast	**fast**
good	**well**
hard	**hard**

Time linkers

We use time linkers when we describe past actions or tell stories:
I was at home **when** he rang.
When he rang, I was at home.
I went to the shopping centre. **Then** I watched a film at the cinema.
I went to the shopping centre **and then** watched a film at the cinema.
Before lunch, I did my homework.
I did my homework **before** lunch.
After school, I went swimming.
I went swimming **after** school.

MODULE 5: LANGUAGE CHOICE 37–42

PRACTICE

37 Exercise **Use the words in brackets to complete the sentences.**

1 I do sport _twice_ a week. (two)
2 I don't like _____ basketball. (play)
3 I love _____ and _____ . (dance/run)
4 I play tennis _____ a week. (one)
5 I don't like _____ exercise. (do)
6 I do yoga _____ a week. (three)
7 My brother loves _____ and _____ .
   (ride horses/play volleyball)
8 My dad doesn't like _____ or _____ .
   (cycle/walk)

38 Present Continuous **Complete the sentences with the verbs in brackets in the Present Continuous.**

1 They _aren't running_ (not run), they _____
   (walk) very fast.
2 The dog _____ (play) with the ball.
3 Why _____ (the teacher / watch) us?
4 The children _____ (do) judo.
5 _____ (you / do) your homework?
6 I _____ (not chat) with friends, I _____
   (use) Wikipedia for homework.
7 _____ (the players / wear) gloves?

39 Present Continuous **Complete the text with the correct forms of the verbs in the Present Continuous tense.**

Hi Ellen! Listen, I'm in the Nou Camp. No, it's not a club, it's FC Barcelona's football stadium, the most famous stadium in the world! And the game [1] _is starting_ (start). They [2] _____ (play) Valencia today. I'm here with some friends. It's great, the fans [3] _____ (sing), we [4] _____ (eat) and [5] _____ (drink) and we're all very excited. Messi [6] _____ (not play) today but Villa [7] _____ (do) very well ... . Ellen, [8] _____ (you / listen) to me? What [9] _____ (you / do)? Wait, I know that music! You [10] _____ (watch) *The Bold and The Beautiful*! Come on! Switch to a sports channel and watch the game!

40 *too/not enough* **Choose the words to complete the sentences.**

1 That football player is very good but he is
   (*too slow*)/*not slow enough*.
2 Ice hockey is *too dangerous/not dangerous enough*.
3 That runner is *too fast/not fast enough* and he never wins medals.
4 I don't want to play tennis because I am
   too tired/not tired enough.
5 Those classes are interesting but they are
   too cheap/not cheap enough.
6 I want to be in the school team but I am
   too good/not good enough.
7 I can't play basketball very well because I am
   too tall/not tall enough.
8 That is a great tennis racquet but it is
   too expensive/not expensive enough.

41 Multi-part verbs (2) **Complete the dialogue with multi-part verbs.**

A: What are you [1] _up to_ ?
B: I'm playing a computer game.
A: Let's [2] _____ . There's a new club in town.
B: I don't know. I'm not [3] _____ dancing tonight – I'm too tired.
A: Oh, [4] _____ Sue. Our friends from school are going.
B: Okay, [5] _____ here in an hour.

42 Present Continuous: arrangements **Complete the sentences with the verbs in the Present Continuous.**

1 _Are you going_ (you / go) to Paris at the weekend?
2 I _____ (meet) Maggie tonight.
3 We _____ (not go) to the cinema on Saturday, we _____ (have) dinner at the new restaurant.
4 _____ (your brother / come) to the party?
5 My friends _____ (not play) a game this afternoon. They _____ (practise) in the gym.
6 We can't meet in the evening, I _____ (do) yoga at 7 p.m..

REFERENCE

Exercise

*I do sport **twice a week**. I **don't like playing football** but I **like swimming** and I **love playing table tennis**. I **am not very fit** and I never **walk up the stairs**. I always **take the lift**.*
*I do sport **five times a week**. I **am very fit** and I always **walk to school**. I never **go by car**.*

Present Continuous
We use the Present Continuous to talk about activities happening:

- now (at the moment).
  *Look, the game **is beginning**!*
  *It's **not raining**.*
  *What **are you doing**?*
- around now.
  *I'm **reading** a lot about disabled athletes.*
  ***Are you studying** European history?*
  *He's **not learning** English.*

We also use the Present Continuous to talk about future events when we have arranged them:
*We're **going** to the theatre tonight. (We've got the tickets.)*
*I'm **starting** a new job in autumn. (I have arranged it.)*

Affirmative	
*I'm **reading**.*	
*He/She/It **is running**.*	
*We/You/They **are working** on a project.*	
Negative	
*I'm **not reading** now.*	
*He/She/It **isn't running** very fast.*	
*We/You/They **aren't helping** them.*	
Questions	**Short answers**
***Are** you **watching** football?*	*Yes, I **am**. / No, **I'm not**.*
***Is** he/she/it **running**?*	*Yes, he/she/it is. / No, he/she/it isn't.*
***Are** we/you/they **helping** him?*	*Yes, we/you/they **are**. / No, we/you/they **aren't**.*
*What **are** you **doing**?*	

too/not enough

*That computer game is **too slow**.*
*That computer game is **not fast enough**.*
*I like basketball but I am **too short**.*
*I like basketball but I am **not tall enough**.*
*We can't play football at home because our garden is **too small**.*
*We can't play football at home because our garden is **not big enough**.*

Multi-part verbs (2)

A: *Do you want to **go out**?*
B: *No, I'm too tired.*

A: *What are you **up to**?*
B: *I'm doing my homework.*

A: *Do you like football?*
B: *No, **I'm not into** playing football.*

A: *Do you want to play my new computer game?*
B: *Yes, I haven't got it.*

A: ***Come round** to my house at four o'clock.*

A: *Let's go skateboarding.*
B: *No, I'm too busy.*
A: *Oh, **come on**, Lucy. It's a fantastic day.*

MODULE 6: LANGUAGE CHOICE 43-48

PRACTICE

43 Describing people **Match the words with the descriptions.**

bus driver   kind   office worker   moody
primary school student   vet   ~~talkative~~
hard-working

1 This person talks a lot. _talkative_
2 This person drives a bus. _____
3 This person works with animals. _____
4 This person goes to primary school. _____
5 This person works hard. _____
6 This person often gets angry. _____
7 This person works in an office. _____
8 This person helps people. _____

44 Present Simple and Continuous **Complete the sentences with the verbs in the Present Simple or Continuous.**

1 You're always tired in the morning. _Do you sleep_ (you / sleep) well?
2 I can't go out now. I _____ (write) an essay.
3 Ronaldo _____ (not play) very well this season.
4 Our neighbour is a teacher. He _____ (work) at my school.
5 Hi Jane, where _____ (you / go)?
6 I _____ (not like) soap operas. They are boring.
7 Come in, Mark. We _____ (have) dinner. Would you like to eat with us?
8 Your sister is vegetarian. _____ (she / eat) fish?

45 Present Simple and Continuous **Complete the text with the verbs in the Present Simple or Continuous.**

My sister, Mary, has a job in London. She ¹_works_ (work) very hard. I and my family ²_____ (live) in a small town and usually Mary ³_____ (not come) home very often. But now she's got her holidays and she ⁴_____ (stay) with us for a week. She ⁵_____ (sleep) in her old room. We ⁶_____ (go) for long walks and in the evening she ⁷_____ (visit) her old friends. She ⁸_____ (like) our town and I think she ⁹_____ (not feel) very comfortable in a big city.

46 Modifiers **Choose adverbs to complete the sentences.**

1 I think that singer is *very/not very* good. He can't sing very well.
2 I think that book is *quite/really* interesting. It's my favourite book.
3 He is *very/not very* old. He is eighty-seven next year.
4 She plays hockey *very/quite* well but she is not in the school team and she is very slow.
5 He is *very/quite* talkative. He never stops talking!
6 That guy is *very/quite* tall but three or four people in the class are taller than him.

47 Information about people **Complete the sentences.**

1 I've got a friend from _the USA_.
2 My brother is a student _____ London University.
3 He's the person _____ short, dark hair.
4 She's the woman _____ the red T-shirt.
5 He is a person _____ a friendly personality.
6 He is a teacher _____ Scotland.

48 Questions **Write two questions for each sentence to ask about the underlined information.**

Mike sleeps nine hours every night.

1 _Who sleeps nine hours every night?_
2 _____

I visit my grandparents every weekend.

3 _____
4 _____

Old people often watch soap operas.

5 _____
6 _____

My grandmother often goes to the cinema because she's got a lot of free time.

7 _____
8 _____

16

REFERENCE

Describing people

*My Aunt Alison is a **pensioner**. She is **seventy years old**. She was a **nurse** at a local hospital. Her husband was a **bus driver**. She is **interested in** music and can play the piano. She is **very clever** and **hard-working**. My brother is a **teenager** and he is **sixteen years old**. He is a **secondary school student**. He wants to be a **doctor**. He is **interested in** sport and likes playing rugby. He is very **outgoing** and **relaxed** - too relaxed! He doesn't like studying.*
*My sister Georgina is a **child**. She is **eight years old**. She is a **primary school student**. She is **very talkative** and **not very tidy**. She is sometimes **moody**.*
*My cousin is **twenty-eight years old**. He is an **engineer** and works in London. His girlfriend is an **office worker**. He is **interested in** reading and loves books. He is very **shy** and **nervous** but he is very **kind**.*

Present Simple and Present Continuous

We use the Present Simple to talk about things that happen regularly or are always true:
*My sister **speaks** three languages.*
*I **don't get up** early.*
***Do** teenagers **need** a lot of sleep?*

We use the Present Continuous to talk about things happening now or around now:
*I**'m watching** my favourite programme.*
*We**'re learning** Spanish.*
***Are** you **staying** in a hotel?*

Compare the sentences:
*I **watch** soap operas.* (I do it regularly because I like them)
*I**'m watching** a soap opera.* (I'm doing it right now, I'm in front of the TV)

Modifiers

*That film is **really** good. I love it.*
*She is **very** old. She is ninety-three.*
*I am **quite** interested in sport. I play football twice a week.*
*He is **not very** friendly. He never talks to people.*

Information about people

*Anthony is a teenager **from** Bristol.*
*He is a person **with** a friendly personality*
*He is a student **at** Bristol University.*
*He is the guy **in** jeans and a blue T-shirt.*
*He is the person **with** short blond hair.*

Questions

***Yes/No* questions start with an auxiliary verb:**
***Do** old people sleep less?*
***Are** you happy?*
***Was** the oldest person in the world Chinese?*

Wh- questions start with question words:
***What** are you interested in?* (to ask about things)
***Where** do old people go on holiday?* (to ask about places)
***Why** are you sad?* (to ask about reasons)
***When** do you visit your grandparents?* (to ask about time)
***Who** did you see?* (to ask about people)
***How** old are you?*

Questions about the subject start with *Who* or *What*. The word order is like in an affirmative sentence:
***Who** speaks English?*
***What**'s happening?*

Compare the questions about the subject and object:
Maria (subject) *likes horror films* (object).
Who likes horror films? Maria.
What does Maria like? Horror films.

PRACTICE

49 **Films** What are the types of films below?

1 They are very romantic and funny, too.
Romantic comedies

2 They are about life in the future. _____ films

3 A lot of people are scared when they watch these films. _____ films

4 They are about real things (e.g. the lives of animals). _____

5 They have lots of action scenes and special effects. _____ films

6 The stories are about cowboys in America. _____

50 *be going to* Order the words to make sentences with *be going to*.

1 take / When / the / are / going / you / to / photo?
When are you going to take the photo?

2 They / see / going / this / are / not / to / film
_____

3 going / Is / be / he / an / to / actor?
_____

4 Hollywood / essay / I / write / going / to / an / am / about
_____

5 to / are / We / going / photography / learn
_____

6 Star Wars / My / is / to / grandmother / going / watch
_____

51 *be going to* Complete the dialogues with the verbs in brackets and *be going to*.

A: The weather is beautiful today. I ¹*'m going to take* (take) some photos in the park.
B: Great idea but let's hurry up. Dad ²_____ (need) the camera tonight.

A: There are some new films in cinemas this weekend. What ³_____ (we / see)?
B: Let's see *Dracula*.
A: Oh, no, I hate horror films. I ⁴_____ (not watch) this film.

A: I broke my brother's camera.
B: What ⁵_____ (you / do)?
A: I ⁶_____ (buy) him a new camera.

52 *like* and *would like* Choose the correct phrase to complete the sentences.

1 I *like*/would like to stay at home and relax tonight.

2 I *don't like*/would like to watching romantic comedies.

3 My teacher *likes*/would like to showing us documentaries in class.

4 A lot of people *like*/would like to go to the Cannes Film Festival.

5 I *don't like*/wouldn't like to eating popcorn when I go to the cinema.

6 I *like*/would like to meet Johnny Depp because he's my favourite actor.

53 *-ed/-ing* adjectives Choose the correct words to complete the description.

I am very ¹*interested*/interesting in photography and I have got a good camera. For me, photography is very ²*relaxed/relaxing*. When I feel ³*tired/tiring* in the evening, I sometimes go out with my camera and take photos. Photography is never ⁴*bored/boring* and I like taking photos of sport. On Saturday, I went to a football match. The game was very ⁵*excited/exciting* and I got some great photos. But I have a problem - my girlfriend doesn't like sport and she gets ⁶*bored/boring* when I show her my photos!

54 *(not) have to* Complete the text with *have to/not have to* and the verbs in brackets.

This summer I'm working on the film set with some friends. We ¹*have to get up* (get up) very early because the work starts at 6 a.m. Actors are more lucky - they ²_____ (not arrive) on the film set before 8 a.m.. I'm working in the canteen: I ³_____ (make) tea and coffee. I ⁴_____ (not prepare) the food but I ⁵_____ (bring) the drinks for the actors and the director. My friend Janet is in the costume crew: she ⁶_____ (carry) clothes and help the actors. She ⁷_____ (not work) very hard but she ⁸_____ (be) very careful because the costumes are expensive.

REFERENCE

Films

*My favourite types of films are **horror films**, **science fiction films** and **thrillers** but I don't like **romantic comedies**. My favourite **director** is James Cameron. My favourite film is Avatar because it has got great **animation** and **special effects**.*

*My favourite types of films are **comedies** and **romantic comedies** but I don't like **documentaries**. My favourite **actor** is Hugh Grant. My favourite film is Love Actually because it has got a great **story** and **funny dialogues**.*

*My favourite types of films are **action** and **fantasy films** but I don't like **westerns**. My favourite **actress** is Angelina Jolie. My favourite film is Tomb Raider because it has got great **action scenes** and **brilliant photography**.*

be going to

We use *be going to* + infinitive to talk about intentions:
*I**'m going to film** my sister's wedding.*
*We**'re not going to stay** at home.*
*What **are you going to do** tonight?*

We can use these time adverbials with *be going to*:
next week / next month / next year / next summer
in two days / in two months' time / in six weeks' time

like and would like

We use *like/don't like* to talk about general preferences:
*I **like watching** films at home. (like + -ing)*
*I **don't like going** to the cinema with my sister.*
(don't like + -ing)
We use *would like* to talk about specific preferences:
*I **would like to go** to the cinema tonight.*
*I **would like to stay** at home and relax.*
(would like + to + infinitive)

-ed/-ing adjectives

We use *-ed* adjectives to describe people's feelings:
*It's been a very long day. I feel really **tired**.*
*I'm playing in the school basketball team tomorrow. I'm really **excited**.*
*I'm on holiday and I'm at the swimming pool. I'm really **relaxed**.*
*I'm **interested** in South American films.*
*I don't like long films with no action. I get very **bored**.*

We use *-ing* adjectives to describe situations or things:
*Zumba classes are very **tiring**.*
*That film has got lots of action scenes – it's very **exciting**.*
*Yoga is very **relaxing** and good for you.*
*That documentary about kangaroos in Australia is very **interesting**.*
*That film is really slow and **boring**.*

have to/not have to

We use *have to* to talk about obligations, to say that something is necessary:
*Actors **have to** listen to the director.*
*I **have to** work in the afternoons.*
*My sister **has to** get up very early.*

We use *not have to* to say that something is not necessary:
*I **don't have to** study today, I haven't got any homework.*
*My brother is lucky – he **doesn't have to** go to school.*
*At my school, we **don't have to** wear uniforms.*

MODULE 8: LANGUAGE CHOICE 55-60

PRACTICE

55 Food **Complete the sentences.**

1 I usually eat a lot of _vegetables_ and my favourite one is broccoli.
2 My favourite _____ is Sunday lunch because we have it with our grandparents.
3 I eat a lot of _____ , like salmon and sardines.
4 My favourite _____ is beef and I don't like chicken.
5 For _____ at 8.00 in the morning, I have cereals and orange _____ .

56 *will/won't* **Use the cues to write predictions and questions about the future.**

1 vegetables / be very expensive
   Vegetables will be very expensive.
2 people / not eat less
   _____
3 children / be overweight?
   _____
4 we / not buy food in supermarkets
   _____
5 shops / sell ready meals?
   _____
6 people / be interested in cooking?
   _____
7 schools / teach about healthy eating
   _____
8 we / live longer
   _____

57 *will/won't* **Complete the dialogue with the verbs in brackets and *will* or *won't*.**

A: So what can you see in the cards? What [1] _will happen_ (happen) to me in the future?
B: You [2] _____ (become) a waiter.
A: What?! I want to be a model!
B: You [3] _____ (not be) a model. But you [4] _____ (have) some money and your restaurant [5] _____ (be) very popular.
A: [6] _____ (my girlfriend / work) with me?
B: No, she [7] _____ . She [8] _____ (write) books about food.
A: [9] _____ (we / be) fat?
B: You [10] _____ (eat) fantastic food but don't worry, you [11] _____ (not be) fat.

58 Confusing words **Choose the correct word to complete the sentences.**

1 I had *lunch*/*a snack* when I was on the bus of an apple and four biscuits.
2 My favourite Spanish *dish*/*meal* is paella.
3 A lot of Japanese *food*/*meal* is very healthy.
4 My favourite *food*/*meal* is dinner.
5 I want to learn to make Italian *dishes*/*meals* like risotto and lasagna.
6 You can buy organic *food*/*dishes* at that shop, like organic fruit and vegetables.

59 *because/because of* **Complete the description with *because* or *because of*.**

I am tired [1] _because of_ that party in a club last night. It was a great party [2] _____ the music. I danced a lot [3] _____ I was with my girlfriend. We had a snack after the party [4] _____ we were hungry. We went to that new café [5] _____ it's near the club but we only had one sandwich [6] _____ the price.

60 Present Conditional **Complete the Present Conditionals with the correct forms of the verbs in brackets.**

1 If you _eat_ (eat) only organic food, _you don't eat_ (not eat) any chemicals.
2 Vegetables _____ (not lose) minerals when they _____ (be) frozen.
3 I _____ (feel) horrible if I _____ (not have) breakfast.
4 If you _____ (drink) coffee in the evening, you _____ (not sleep) well at night.
5 People _____ (be) stressed, if they _____ (work) a lot.
6 When I _____ (cook) at home, I know that the food _____ (be) healthy.

REFERENCE

Food

I usually eat a lot of *cereals*. I love *bread*, *rice* and *pasta*, too.

I usually eat a lot of *vegetables,* like *broccoli*, *cabbage* and *lettuce*.

I sometimes eat fish, like *tuna*, *sardines* and *salmon*.

I sometimes eat *cheese*, *eggs* and *yoghurt*.

I sometimes eat *meat,* like *chicken*, *beef* and *lamb* but I never eat *pork*.

I don't eat a lot of *fruit*. I never eat *apples* and I sometimes eat *oranges*.

I drink a lot of *orange juice* and *tea* but I don't like *coffee* and *cola*.

My favourite *meal* is *lunch*. I have a small *breakfast* and *dinner*.

I often eat snacks, like *sweets* and *chocolates*.

I sometimes eat *crisps* and *biscuits*, too.

will/won't

We use *will/won't* to make predictions about the future:

Food *will be* more expensive next year.

You *will love* my pasta.

Don't worry, you *won't get* ill.

I'm afraid he *won't cook* lunch.

We use these time expressions with *will/won't*:

tomorrow (He*'ll come tomorrow*.)

next week/month/year (Strawberries *won't be* very cheap *next year*.)

in two weeks' time, in three months' time, in two years' time (Junk food *will disappear* in *twenty years' time*.)

After *will* and *won't* we always use infinitive without *to*:

Affirmative	
People *will cook* at home. There *will be* more healthy food.	
Negative	
There *won't be* many fat people. We *won't eat* sweets.	
Questions	**Short answers**
Will supermarkets still *be* popular? Where *will* people *buy* food?	Yes, they *will*. / No, they *won't*.

Confusing words

Food: things that you eat.

I like Chinese food and I love Italian food.

Meal: a time when you eat food.

Why don't you come for a meal on Saturday?

Dish: food cooked in a particular way.

Lasagne is an Italian dish.

Snack: a very small meal.

I often have a snack after swimming, usually some biscuits and an apple.

because/because of

because of + noun:

I don't like that hotel because of the food.

I didn't have lunch because of the time.

You can't go on the roof because of the bees.

because + noun/pronoun + verb:

I don't like that hotel because the food there is not very good.

I didn't have lunch because I didn't have time.

You can't go on the roof because there are bees on it.

Present Conditional

We use the Present Conditional to talk about rules, when one event or situation always follows another event or situation:

People get fat if they eat a lot of sweets.

If I don't exercise, I feel bad.

In these sentences if = when:

* We use the pattern: *If/When* + Present Simple, Present Simple

MODULE 9: LANGUAGE CHOICE 61-66

PRACTICE

61 **My country Complete the description of a country. What is the country?**

My ¹ _country_ is quite big (for Europe) with more than 500,000 square kilometres. The ²_____ is forty-seven million. Our ³_____ city is Madrid and I live there. In the ⁴_____ , it is sometimes quite cold and snowy. In the ⁵_____ , it is usually very sunny and hot - sometimes it is 40° in August! In the north, there are some lovely forests and national ⁶_____ . In the south and east, there are some fantastic beaches.

62 **a/an Complete the sentences with a/an or -.**

1: I'm interested in ¹_-_ science. I'd like to study ²_____ maths at ³_____ American university.
2: We went to ⁴_____ nice café in Rome. I had ⁵_____ omelette and Dave had ⁶_____ spaghetti.
3: I'm in ⁷_____ film club at school. We're watching ⁸_____ Chinese and Japanese films this month.
4: I've got ⁹_____ friend in the United States. He works in ¹⁰_____ fast food restaurant and sells ¹¹_____ hamburgers. I'm reading ¹²_____ interesting book about ¹³_____ Asian students in Europe.

63 **a/an/the Complete the text with a/an, the or -.**

My father is ¹_a_ doctor and he works in ²_____ hospital and my mother is ³_____ journalist - she works for ⁴_____ magazine. They love ⁵_____ travelling. Every year we spend ⁶_____ holidays in ⁷_____ different country. Last year we went to India and we loved ⁸_____ country and ⁹_____ people. ¹⁰_____ weather was very nice - we were in ¹¹_____ north of India so it wasn't very hot and ¹²_____ nights were cold. We liked ¹³_____ food, too. We usually had ¹⁴_____ sandwiches for ¹⁵_____ lunch but in the evening, we had ¹⁶_____ dinner in ¹⁷_____ local restaurant. And every morning, we had ¹⁸_____ cup of ¹⁹_____ Indian tea - it's strong, sweet and they make it with ²⁰_____ milk and ²¹_____ spices.

64 **Travel Complete the description of the holiday.**

We went ¹ _by_ bus to the airport and went to Costa Rica by ²_____ . In Costa Rica, we travelled around ³_____ car. We stayed on the Pacific coast and every day went swimming and ⁴_____ - the water was great! Then we went ⁵_____ in the mountains - one day we walked twenty-five kilometres. We saw lots of interesting animals, like the ⁶_____ . It is similar to a big monkey and it is very, very slow! Then we went ⁷_____ in San José and saw a lot of old buildings and churches.

65 **Nationality adjectives Complete the sentences with nationality adjectives.**

1 Galatasaray and Besiktas are _Turkish_ football teams.
2 Paella is a _____ dish.
3 San Francisco is an _____ city.
4 Toyota and Nissan cars are _____ .
5 Renaults and Peugeots are _____ cars.
6 Inter Milan is an _____ football team.

66 **Indefinite pronouns Complete the dialogue with indefinite pronouns.**

A: It's late, Bill, we have to go.
B: I can't see my passport ¹ _anywhere_ .
A: It's ²_____ on your desk. Have you got the maps and guide books?
B: Yes, I've got ³_____ , even a Dutch-English phrase book.
A: The phrase book is not necessary. ⁴_____ speaks English in Amsterdam. Have you got ⁵_____ to read on the plane?
B: No, I haven't. And I've got ⁶_____ to eat.
A: Don't worry, we can eat ⁷_____ at the airport.

REFERENCE

My country

My country is quite small.
The population is sixty-two million.
Our capital city is London.
In the winter, it is sometimes quite **cold** and **snowy**.
In the spring, it is often **windy** and **rainy**.
In the summer, it is sometimes **sunny** but often **cloudy**.
In the autumn, it is often **foggy** and **windy**.
In the west, there are some **beautiful beaches**.
In the north, there are some **lovely forests**.
In Scotland, there are some **beautiful mountains**.

a/an/the

We use *a/an* in front of singular countable nouns. We use *an* in front of nouns that start with a vowel:
a book / *a* window
an actress / *an* exam

We use *a* when we talk about one of many people or things and it doesn't matter which one precisely we are talking about or when we talk about the person or thing for the first time:
We need *a* car. (I'm not thinking about a specific car)
I've got *a* friend. He lives in Amsterdam. (We talk about this person for the first time)

We use *the* when we talk about something unique or when the other person knows who/what we are talking about:
The sun is shining. (we know only one sun)
The professor says I am his best student. (my professor)
Feed *the* dog. She is hungry. (our dog)

There are a lot of phrases without articles:
at night, at home, at school, in hospital, in bed,
by train, by plane, by taxi,
go to school, go to work, go home,
before lunch, after dinner,
have breakfast, have lunch

Travel

Transport
I go to school **by bus**. My dad goes to work **by bike**. My mum goes to work **by car**. We go on holiday **by plane**.

Holiday activities
We sometimes **go hiking** in the forest or **white-water rafting** on the river. When I go to the beach, I **go swimming and surfing**. When I went to London last year, we **went sightseeing**.

Animals
crocodile, elephant, giraffe, lion, monkey, sloth, turtle

Nationality adjectives

+ an
America - Americ**an**, Argentina - Argentin**ian**,
Australia - Austral**ian**, Brazil - Brazil**ian**,
Bulgaria - Bulgar**ian**, Canada - Canad**ian**, Chile - Chil**ean**,
Colombia - Colomb**ian**, Croatia - Croat**ian**,
Germany - Germ**an**, Hungary - Hungar**ian**,
Italy - Ital**ian**, Lithuania - Lithuan**ian**,
Mexico - Mexic**an**, Peru - Peru**vian**,
Romania - Roman**ian**, Russia - Russ**ian**,
Serbia - Serb**ian**, Slovakia - Slovak**ian**,
South Africa - South Afric**an**,
Ukraine - Ukrain**ian**, Uruguay - Uruguay**an**

+ ish
Britain - Brit**ish**, Denmark - Dan**ish**, Ireland - Ir**ish**, Poland - Pol**ish**, Scotland - Scott**ish**, Spain - Span**ish**, Sweden - Swed**ish**, Turkey - Turk**ish**

+ ese
China - Chin**ese**, Japan - Japan**ese**, Portugal - Portug**uese**

irregular
Czech Republic - **Czech**, France - **French**, Greece - **Greek**, the Netherlands - **Dutch**, Switzerland - **Swiss**, New Zealand - **New Zealand/New Zealander**, Wales - **Welsh**

Indefinite pronouns

We use *someone, anyone, everyone* and *no one* to talk about people.
We use *something, anything, nothing* and *everything* to talk about things.
We use *somewhere, anywhere, everywhere* and *nowhere* to talk about places.

We usually use the pronouns that begin with *some* (*someone, something, somewhere*) in affirmative sentences:
Someone showed us the way.
We left the car *somewhere* here.

We usually use the pronouns that begin with *any* (*anyone, anything, anywhere*) in questions and negative sentences:
I can't see *anyone*!
Is there *anything* to do in Warsaw?

No one, nothing, nowhere have negative meaning - if they appear in a sentence, we do not use negation:
No one likes moody people.
There's *nothing* to eat.

We use all indefinite pronouns with singular verbs:
Everyone is in the museum.
There is *no one* in the street.

PRACTICE

67 Gadgets Complete the description with the words below.

download   online (x 2)   use   smart
~~into~~   upload   check

I am ¹ _into_ technology – I love it! When I get up, I go ² _____ and ³ _____ my emails and messages. I always take my ⁴ _____ phone to school and read articles and blogs on the bus. After lunch, I ⁵ _____ Facebook and I ⁶ _____ photos from my digital camera. In the evening, I play ⁷ _____ computer games and ⁸ _____ films to watch.

68 Present Perfect Complete the sentences with the verbs in brackets in the Present Perfect tense.

1 My father _has bought_ (buy) a lot of gadgets in his life.
2 My friends _____ (not use) a smart phone.
3 I _____ (write) twenty emails today.
4 My sister _____ (not see) *The Pirates of the Caribbean*.
5 My school _____ (have) six head teachers.
6 I _____ (not lose) anything in my life.
7 My grandmother _____ (work) in different countries.
8 I'm sorry, you _____ (not win) the competition.

69 never Order the words to write sentences in the Present Perfect. Put *never* in the correct places.

1 I / uploaded / my photos / have / never
   I have never uploaded my photos.
2 We / talked / have / about / our families / never
3 Our neighbours / sent / us / have/ an email / never
4 You / never / learned / have / Spanish
5 My English teacher / showed / us / never / a film / has
6 I / Africa / been / to / have / never
7 You / my sister / met / never / have
8 My sister / the guitar / has / played / never

70 have Complete the sentences.

1 My friend had a _party_ last week. There were fifty people and the food was great!
2 She had _____ at school because she was online all night and only slept two hours.
3 I have _____ at nine o'clock in the morning at the weekend – I usually have eggs and an orange juice.
4 Susan's parties are always fantastic – I always have _____ with her friends and we dance a lot.

71 Indirect object Complete the sentences with the words below.

me   my girlfriend   my dog
him   us   ~~the teacher~~

1 Ask _the teacher_ a question about the exam. You are seeing her tomorrow.
2 Please, send _____ a message about your holiday. I want to know about it!
3 My brother is very happy. My grandma gave _____ a new net book for his birthday.
4 He was very hungry so I gave _____ a biscuit.
5 Our teacher gave _____ a lot of homework for next week.
6 Yesterday, I gave _____ a book because she loves reading.

72 Present Perfect: questions Use the cues to complete the dialogue with questions in the Present Perfect.

A: ¹ _Have you ever had a computer_ (you / ever / have a computer)?
B: No, I haven't.
A: ² _____ (you / ever / use a mobile phone)?
B: Yes, I have. My sister's mobile.
A: ³ _____ (your sister / ever / lend you / her laptop)?
B: No, she hasn't. ⁴ _____ (your brother / ever / give you his PSP)?
A: No, he hasn't. He thinks I'll break it.